REVELATIONS OF JESUS CHRIST

REVELATIONS OF JESUS CHRIST

REVELATIONS
OF JESUS CHRIST

from the book of Revelation

– a devotional study –

PHILIP WREN

Christian Publications International

First published in Great Britain by
Christian Publications International
an imprint of
Buy Research Ltd., Salisbury House, Station Road, Cambridge, CB1 2LA

Scripture quotations are taken from the New King James Version®.
Copyright © 1982 by Thomas Nelson, Inc. Used by permission. All rights reserved.

www.christian-publications-int.com

Readers are encouraged to compare assertions in all CPI books with the clear witness of Scripture. CPI offers this book as a contribution towards continuing study of the inspired Word of God, which the publisher considers to be the final 'court of appeal' in matters of faith and doctrine.

ISBN 978-1-78926-511-8

Printed in Great Britain by Imprint Digital, Exeter
and worldwide by CreateSpace.

REVELATIONS OF JESUS CHRIST

REVELATIONS OF JESUS CHRIST

PREFACE

"The Greeks learned in order to comprehend.
The Hebrews learned in order to revere.
The modern man learns in order to use."
Abraham Joshua Heschel

This book has been written with the primary purpose
of causing people to revere our wonderful Saviour.
In reading it you will gain some knowledge
and in the years to come that knowledge will prove useful.
But the main purpose in preparing these studies
is to glorify Jesus.
It aims to inspire greater love for Him as our Messiah
and encourage us to be ready for His return.

REVELATIONS OF JESUS CHRIST

INTRODUCTION

A Revelation of Jesus Christ, which God gave Him to show His servants things which must shortly take place." Revelation 1: 1.

The opening words of the book of Revelation confirm its purpose. It is 'a revelation of Jesus Christ'. The Son does not glorify Himself. It is His Father who reveals His Son, so that we can give to Jesus the glory due. He is a Son who, in perfect humility, submission and obedience, has brought about the salvation of mankind.

The Son is central to all that follows. The future, our future, is entirely bound up in Him. If we want to understand the things which must shortly take place we need to understand Jesus Christ. Therefore as we come to study Revelation our primary question is; 'what does this book reveal about Jesus?'

The following studies bring different insights into the character of Jesus. Some revelations confirm what has gone before, others occur nowhere else in scripture.

One day all of heaven and earth will bow before Jesus Christ. Revelation is a foretaste of the glory which belongs to Him alone.

A secondary purpose of Revelation is to encourage us to persevere in the face of opposition and so become **overcomers**. We persevere because our trust is in the Saviour revealed in the pages of this book. The more we understand His glory the greater our assurance that in Him our hope is secure.

The teaching of Revelation applies to every age but especially for those living at the end of the age. It brings encouragement to those facing persecution and martyrdom. It also warns sinners of the inevitability of judgement.

Note on the author

Revelation is a book which comes from the highest authority. The introduction states that its originator is God the Father. It was transmitted via the Son, then by an angel to John who wrote down what was revealed.

The writer is introduced as *John*. The early church fathers attribute Revelation to the Apostle John[1]. It was written towards the end of the first century when John was about 90 years old and imprisoned on the island of Patmos.

Revelation 1: 1 – 3

"Blessed is he who reads and those who hear the words of this prophecy, and keep those things which are written in it; for the time is near."

The book opens with a blessing for those who both read and act on what is written in it. It closes with a warning that to add or take away from it endangers losing our place in the Holy City.

The study of Revelation brings many blessings. The first is a greater insight into the character of our wonderful Saviour. The next blessing is an understanding that despite the turmoil of the world, Jesus is in control and working out His purposes. Then there is an assurance that those who are persecuted or martyred do not suffer in vain. It is a great blessing to look ahead to the promise of the wedding feast and have a glimpse of the glory that lies ahead for those who put their trust in Jesus.

The assurance that Jesus has already won the victory over Satan will also bless the reader. The final overthrow of Satan and ejection from this world is just a matter of time.

Seven times in Revelation those who keep the faith are referred to as blessed.

---

[1] The early church generally accepted him (John) as the apostle of Jesus Christ, the author of the Fourth Gospel. This was clearly attested as early as A.D. 150 by Justin Martyr and around A.D. 200 by Irenaeus." 'Commentary on the Revelation of John' by George Eldon Ladd.

Those who read and keep what is written in it, (Rev 1: 3).
Those who die in the Lord, (Rev 14: 13).
Those who watch, (Rev 16: 15).
Those invited to the marriage supper of the Lamb, (Rev 19: 9).
Those who are part of the first resurrection, (Rev 20: 6).
Those who keep these words of prophecy, (Rev 22: 7).
Those who do His commands, (Rev 22: 14).

Receiving the blessing requires keeping what the book teaches. Therefore in order to be blessed by it we need to study it.

Besides the blessing, there is an assurance that the time is near. God will delay no longer than necessary to complete His purposes. What may seem a never ending age to us in this life, is a mere blink of an eye when seen in the light of eternity.

Revelation is dramatic with mind blowing imagery. Some are frightened by it, others obsessed by it. I trust that what follows will calm the fears of those who are frightened by the symbolism and imagery. There is nothing to fear for in reality the book is all about Christ. For those who are obsessed by it, I trust that it will keep their eyes focused on the One who is central to all that follows, our Saviour the Lord Jesus Christ. If you have in the past been indifferent to this book, then please read on so that you can receive its blessing.

About this book

Hebrew names of God

Each chapter is headed by a Hebrew name of God. The names are given to summarise the character of Christ as revealed in the chapter which follows. They emphasise that the character of Christ is unchanged from the Old Testament to the New. The names remind us that Revelation concludes not just the New Testament but the whole Bible.

Structure

There are numerous ways in which people understand the structure of the book of Revelation. Some see it a consecutive summary of end time events. Others explain it as a series of parallel visions. In this study it is treated as a series of snap shots each revealing an aspect of the character of Christ.

The Boxes

The boxes are given at the beginning of each chapter to frame each snap shot. They give the portion of the book being studied, the main revelation of Christ being considered and the time frame which the portion covers.

An Introduction

There is a brief introduction to each chapter. It is often in the form of the question which the snap shot answers.

The Text

The main text of the chapter follows. This book can be read as a whole or as a series of individual studies. The short chapters lend themselves to personal study and reflection on the greatness of Jesus the Christ our Saviour.

EL SHADDAI
ALMIGHTY GOD

Almighty in the sense that God is all sufficient. First used in the Bible when God appears to *Abram* to enlarge the covenant (Genesis 17: 1). In the introduction to Revelation Jesus refers to Himself as *the Almighty*. A fitting reassurance for those who are facing suffering and persecution.

REFERENCE	TOPIC	TIMESPAN
Revelation 1: 4–20	**Christ Glorified** A revelation of Jesus Christ in His eternal glory	A day towards the close of the first century AD.

In your mind, how do you picture Jesus Christ? Is He the humble carpenter from Nazareth wandering the hills of Galilee and Judea with His band of disciples? Do you picture Him teaching the people and feeding the five thousand? Maybe you see Him healing the sick and casting out demons. Perhaps it is the confrontations with the religious rulers which comes to mind. Then there is His suffering on the cross.

We are comforted that in the gospels He is very human. He is like a very kind older brother. It is reassuring that the One who intercedes for us in heaven once lived among men on earth.

That is the Christ of history. The person we will one day meet is very different. In the book of Revelation, the encounter we have with *Jesus the Messiah* introduces us to **how He is now**. The vision is both very powerful and slightly disturbing.

Christ Glorified

Revelation 1: 4 - 20

John records that he was in the Spirit *on the Lord's Day*. Early on, Christians started meeting on the first day of the week (Acts 20:7,

1 Corinthians 16: 2). However it was not until later, in the second century AD, that the first day of the week became referred to as *the Lord's Day*. Some translations read *"In the Spirit on the Imperial Day"*. In the context of Revelation this is probably a better translation. On *the Imperial Day* all the peoples of the Roman Empire were required to swear allegiance to the Roman Emperor as Lord. Refusal to worship Caesar as Lord could result in exile or death.

Revelation was given during the reign of the **Emperor Domitian** (81-96 AD). Obsessed with his own deity, Domitian insisted on being called "Lord and God". The cult of Emperor Worship was viciously applied, especially in Asia Minor. It was the Roman way of unifying the empire. You could have your own gods but the emperor had to be one of them. On this day, many whom John knew and loved, were under intense pressure to renounce their faith and worship Caesar.

While John is interceding for those he loved, the Lord brings this message of encouragement for the churches of Asia. The grounds for that encouragement are set out in the brief introduction. The words of this introduction, supported by other scriptures confirm the nature of Christ.

1) Jesus Christ is:

'the faithful witness'.

A reminder that Jesus became one of us and suffered for us. *"He humbled himself and became obedient to death, even death on the cross"* Philippians 2: 8. He knows what it is like to suffer and to be tempted but not give up (Hebrews 2: 18). He asks less of us than he went through Himself.

'the first born of the dead'.

It is an encouragement to know that whatever this life brings, we have a glorious future. Because Jesus was raised from the dead we can be sure that we will be raised also (1 Corinthians 15: 20).

'the ruler of the kings of the earth'.

Jesus has won the victory. He is now sovereign. Power can only be exercised on earth with His permission (Ephesians 1: 20 – 22).

2) 'To Him who loves us'.

He loves us whatever our outward circumstances. However dark our situation we cannot be separated from His love (Romans 8: 35 -39).

'and washed us from our sins by His own blood'.

We are forgiven, not because of our efforts but due to His sacrifice. If it were by our own efforts, we would always question if we had done enough to earn His forgiveness (Ephesians 1: 7).

'and has made us kings and priests'.

The world may despise us but whatever the world may think, our status is settled. We are now in royal service. Israel was the first to be called a kingdom of priests (Exodus 19: 6). Later this is also applied to the church (1 Peter 2: 9).

'Behold, He is coming with clouds'.

He is coming again to judge the world. Those who have suffered for Jesus in this life will soon be rewarded. (2 Thessalonians 1: 6 – 10). Israel will repent and receive her Saviour. (Zechariah 12: 10).

For the Christian the return of Christ will be pure joy, but the world will mourn when He appears. The return of Christ will be the ultimate disaster. They will know that the one so long scorned has returned as the Judge.

3) 'I am the Alpha and the Omega'

The first and last letters of the Greek alphabet stress that Jesus is the beginning and the end, the first and the last. Everything that exists comes from Him (John 1: 3). He is both Lord of human history and the One who determines the future.

4) 'The Almighty'

God revealed Himself to Abram as *El Shaddai, God Almighty*

(Genesis 17: 1). He is eternal, all powerful and all sufficient. The grounds for our encouragement are encapsulated in the words 'God Almighty'. He is above all powers and principalities. He is the One who brought all things into existence. He is the One who determines the future and guides history to fulfil His plans. No matter what is happening in the world, we can trust Him.

John now sets the context for the vision. He was in exile on the Island of Patmos. Despite being in prison he was "in the Spirit", which we may understand as his being caught up in the worship of God. While in this state of devotion he has an encounter with the risen Lord Jesus.

The Glorified Christ

As John is intently interceding a loud authoritative voice breaks in. John is commanded to write in a book and send it to the seven churches. His prayers are answered with a word for each of these churches which he once cared for. The word is not one of instant relief from the present suffering. Instead John receives an assurance that Jesus cares for each congregation.

John turns and sees seven golden lampstands which we are told represent the seven churches. Among the lampstands is one who John recognises as the 'Son of Man'. The gospels record that Jesus repeatedly referred to Himself as the 'Son of Man'. It is a reference back to Daniel 7: 13, 14 where the Son of Man is *the Messiah*. John would have remembered that, at His trial, when Jesus said He was the 'Son of Man', it condemned Him to the cross. (Matthew 26: 64). The High Priest recognised this title as a claim to be the Messiah and declared the statement to be blasphemy.

The vision now introduces us to the Jesus of the present. This is the Jesus to whom we address our prayers. A long time before this vision, John had briefly glimpsed Christ as He sees Him now. On the mount of transfiguration, Jesus was revealed in His eternal glory (Matthew 17: 2). His glory was also revealed to the prophets *Daniel* (Daniel 10: 5 – 8) and *Ezekiel* (Ezekiel 1: 26- 28).

At the *Last Supper* John records how he lay on Jesus' breast (John 13: 23). Jesus was like a close friend or brother. The glorified Jesus invokes a different response. Ezekiel, Daniel and John all respond in the same way. They fall at His feet as if dead.

'The First and the Last' (v.17)

This is a title of the Lord, the King of Israel. (Isaiah 41:4, 44:6).

This same Jesus, now glorified, still loves and moves among His people. He speaks to the congregations and their shepherds on the state of their faith, commending what is good, and correcting their faults.

He warns us of the dangers of failing to correct things which are going wrong, while at the same time assuring us that He is concerned to ensure that we come through.

For the shepherds of the congregations there is a special encouragement. Jesus doesn't just walk among them. They are held as seven stars in His right hand.

John saw Jesus die. He also saw Jesus after the resurrection. In His resurrection body Jesus was both recognisable and different. In his gospel John wrote, *"Yet none of His disciples dared ask Him, "who are you?" knowing it was the Lord."* John 21: 12. Jesus had been restored by His Father to His former glory. A glory which one day we will share (1John 3: 2). Jesus has conquered death, He is alive for ever more. Because He lives we shall also live, (John 14: 19).

This is the Jesus before whom one day each of us will have to stand and give an account of our lives (Romans 14: 12). Before those eyes of fire nothing is hidden. (Hebrews 4: 12, 13). Like John on that day we will fall at His feet as if dead. There will be no arguments which we can put forward to justify our actions. No explaining away of what we have thought and done.

On that day we will understand as never before that it is by grace that we have been saved through faith, not by works but by the gift of God. (Ephesians 2: 8-9).

Note:

A pattern, repeated throughout Revelation, is to deal with the things of God and the righteous first, then the fate of the unrighteous is described. This follows the priority of God, which is always for His chosen ones. Therefore we start by focusing on the body of believers, then on God and the victory of the Lamb, before considering the conflict in this world. We see the redeemed in the Kingdom of God, before considering the trumpet judgements. The fate of the witnesses and Israel, are described before the kingdom of the beast. The harvest of the righteous is described before the wrath of God is poured out on the wicked. The marriage of the Lamb is set before the overthrow of the Antichrist.

The Lord's Day - Revelation 1: 10

In his interlinear Greek/English New Testament, **Alfred Marshall** translates '*kuriakos*' in Revelation 1:10 as '*imperial*'. In 1 Corinthians 11: 20, the only other place in the New Testament that the word is used, he translates it as '*Lord*' but with a note that it is a Greek adjective for which there is no exact English equivalent.

In *Young's* concordance '*kuriakos*' is assigned the meaning '*belonging to the Lord*'.

It is entirely appropriate that Paul uses '*kuriakos*' in Corinthians. The Corinthian Church was guilty of abusing the Lord's Supper by having no regard for the body of Christ. Paul is emphasizing that it is not a social occasion but a celebration instituted by our Lord. It is His particular celebration when we remember all that He suffered for us. This is the holy ground of the church and the one act of worship which should unite all Christians in our common indebtedness to Jesus Christ. The Lord's Supper is '*kuriakos*', belonging to Him.

The New Testament does not teach that there is a day, which specially belongs to Jesus. If anything we are taught that every day is '*kuriakos*', belonging to Him. This is not to question the principle that setting aside one day for rest and worship is still good for our physical and spiritual wellbeing.

Therefore if there is no day which is '*kuriakos*' in a Christian sense, John was using the term as generally understood in the first century, the *Imperial* or *Emperor's* day.

In the second century Christians started to refer to their day of gathering together for worship as the Lord's Day. Many commentators believe that this developed as an act of defiance. If Caesar can have a day when people are required to worship him, Christians will have a day when they choose to worship Jesus. They chose the first day of the week because it was the day when Jesus was exalted by His resurrection, to sovereignty over all the Kings of the earth, including Caesar.

However if the word should be understood as the 'Lord's Day' i.e.: a Christian Sabbath, it does not greatly alter the meaning, as by this act of defiance they were opening themselves up to persecution.

After praying over this verse I believe that the word *'Imperial'* is correct. John, through intense prayer, was identifying with those he knew and loved. These faithful disciples were, on this day, facing appalling persecution.

REVELATIONS OF JESUS CHRIST

EL ROI
THE GOD WHO SEES

Hagar used this name for God when she ran away from *Sarai* (Genesis 16: 13). God watches over us even in times of affliction. He sees all that is happening in the local congregation of believers.

REFERENCE	TOPIC	TIMESPAN
Revelation 2: 1–29 **Revelation 3: 1–22**	**Christ and His body** A message of discipline and encouragement to the congregations from their Head.	Initially the early church; but also relevant to the period from Pentecost to the Second Coming.

In this study we look at the relationship of Jesus to His body on earth. Has He left us with some written instructions, the promise of the Holy Spirit and told us to get on with it, *or is the relationship more intimate?* Due to overfamiliarity, we can lose sight of the significance of the letters to the seven churches.

In these letters, Jesus reveals Himself to be *intimately* concerned with the affairs and wellbeing of each individual congregation. His care is similar to the Lord's intimacy toward Israel, as revealed through the Old Testament prophets. This is the place in the New Testament where we learn of Christ's heart for His church.

The letters are addressed in the singular to the messenger of the church. The same word, translated as angel or messenger, is used in reference to *John the Baptist* (Matthew 11: 10). Reading the letters it is clear that they are addressed to the person who has pastoral responsibility for the congregation. The *pastor* (Latin for shepherd) is responsible to ensure that his flock receive good food and for protection from those who would destroy. His work, good deeds and failures, will be reflected in the flock.

That is a daunting responsibility! But Jesus has given the assurance that He is holding the seven stars (the shepherds) in the palm of his hand. He will stand with them if they faithfully discharge their calling.

'I know' is repeated seven times, emphasizing the perfect knowledge Jesus has of each congregation. All the letters end with the words *'He who has an ear'*, all have ears but many will not listen.

Each congregation has a partial vision of Christ revealed to them according to their need. The full measure of Christ is revealed if the congregations share their letters. Both the vision and reward for each is different. They relate to each congregation's specific area of warfare.

Christ and His body

Revelation 2: 1 – 7 Ephesus

Ephesus is outwardly a prosperous, successful, active congregation. They have faithfully stood for the truth and exposed false teachers. There is special praise for their exposing the corruption of the Nicolaitans. 'Nicolaitans' is made up of two Greek words 'nikos', *'to have victory or conquer'* and 'laos', *'people'*. Therefore the name could describe a group of people who seek to dominate the followers of Christ and thus destroy the body. Jesus is head of His church. He hates those who seek to usurp His position.

With the appearance of good order and faithfulness, the Ephesians lack one thing: the joy and enthusiasm which arises out of our love for the Lord. This is no trivial matter, for love is central to the congregation. Without it we become no more than *'a noisy gong or a clanging cymbal'* (1 Corinthians 13: 1). In fact without love, a church is of no use to our Lord. It is His love within us and toward the members of His body which witnesses to the world (John 13: 34 – 35). The lampstand represents the presence of the Holy Spirit. If the Holy Spirit is no longer present the church becomes an empty shell. There are many reasons why we can lose our first love. Even the constant defence against false teachers can wear us down.

The answer given by Jesus is repent. We are to stand up for the purity of the church but the motivation must always be; first love for our Lord, second love for His body the church, third compassion for the one who has gone astray and finally concern for the lost.

The promised reward for those who overcome, is to eat from the tree of life. The eternal life which we are promised is sustained by eating the fruit of the tree of life. That fruit enables us to live forever in perfect fellowship with God, as was experienced in the Garden of Eden.

Revelation 2: 8 – 11 Smyrna

Smyrna is a persecuted congregation that has suffered from human and demonic attack. Both the cult of emperor worship and hostility from the Jews were very strong there. Jesus is the First and Last. He reigns far above all human authority. There came a time when He suffered, was dead and buried, and then came alive. It reminds the congregation of Christ's sovereignty and His victory over death.

That the Jews are constantly bringing false accusations against the body is recognized in the term 'synagogue of Satan'. 'Satan' is the Hebrew word for 'accuser'.

Jesus knows that in the ongoing persecution some will give their lives. A repeated call in Revelation is to stand firm in the face of a hostile world. Through persecution Smyrna has been purified. Jesus finds nothing to reprove in them. If they remain faithful unto death they will receive a crown of life. The life that the world takes from us, the Lord will give back in abundance.

The second death is condemnation to the lake of fire. (Revelation 20: 13 – 15). Those who overcome and remain victorious have nothing to fear.

Revelation 2: 12 – 17 Pergamos

Pergamos was known for its three temples dedicated to the worship of the Roman Emperor and a vast altar of **Zeus**. Tradition informs us that **Antipas** refused to declare Caesar as Lord and God. He was sacrificed on the altar of Zeus in 92 AD, which incidentally confirms the date of Revelation.

Despite what happened to Antipas many in the congregation stood firm, but some members advocated compromise. *Balaam* is given as an example of a person corrupted by the love of money. Whereas the Nicolaitans seek to dominate and control, Balaam in return for money (2 Peter 2: 15) seduced Israel to disobey God. Both these groups seek acceptance by the world through the adoption of worldly standards.

People who teach compromise are to repent, or suffer Jesus coming against them. In the vision, Christ has a two edged sword. He will use it to separate truth from falsehood. See also Hebrews 4:12.

Balaam advised *Balak* that to defeat the Israelites he should entice them to worship Moab's god, (Numbers 31: 16). One of Israel's sins was to eat unclean food offered to idols. In contrast, Jesus promises those who stand firm, pure food from God. A new name is a sign of God's blessing.

Revelation 2: 18 – 29 *Thyatira*

Thyatira is the opposite of Ephesus. They are commended for their works of love but condemned for their tolerance. Lacking a sense of the holiness of God, they turn a blind eye to sin. In the vision, Christ has eyes of fire and feet of brass. The eyes of fire search minds and hearts, nothing can be hidden. He sees the corruption which has become rooted in the congregation. The feet of brass will trample on Christ's enemies.

The shepherd of the church at Thyatira has allowed the *Jezebel* to seduce Christ's servants into sin. It seems that some in the congregation have challenged her immorality. She has been warned and given time, but refused to repent.

Jezebel, the wife of *King Ahab,* caused Israel to worship *Baal* and other false gods (1 Kings 16:31, 18:4, 13, 19, 19: 1 – 3, 21: 5 – 23,). Her counterpart in this church has deceived members into the acceptance of other religions and forms of worship, with their accompanying immorality. She has led them astray by teaching that they need to understand the ways (deep things) of Satan. *Gnosticism* taught that in order to defeat Satan, one had to enter his stronghold, i.e.: experience evil deeply. Her sin is a deadly combination of sexual immorality and idolatry. Those who have been led astray by her will be severely judged.

Jesus, whose eyes are like a flame of fire, can see into minds and hearts. Nothing is hidden. He knows our real motives and will reward us accordingly. When He comes to reign it will be with a rod of iron. The rod of iron and shattered clay are quotes from Psalm 2: 9, which refers to that reign. His reign will be benevolent but firm (Isaiah 11: 4 – 5).

Those who have not been led astray are called on to hold fast. They will be rewarded by reigning with Christ. Jesus is the true morning star, herald of the day. (2 Peter 1:19, Revelation 22:16).

Revelation 3: 1 – 6 Sardis

Sardis is about to die. Outwardly she is an active congregation with plenty going on. But her works are not undertaken in obedience to Christ, therefore they are empty.

Both the call to watch and Jesus coming as a thief, are reminders of coming judgment (Luke 21: 36, 1 Thessalonians 5: 2 – 11). The solution to their problems is to repent. The people of Sardis are to remember how they started out. Sardis reminds us how easy it is to lose focus. Perhaps they were looking for numbers attending meetings rather than real conversions.

In Christ our sins are washed away. We are clean. If we fall back into the ways of the world our garments become soiled. Some at Sardis have not soiled their garments, which implies that most have. Those whose garments are not soiled will not have their names blotted out from the Book of Life. Again this implies that those with soiled garments will have their names blotted out. They lose their salvation. Jesus will confess the names of the faithful before His Father, but those whose names are blotted out will be disowned.

At the wedding of the Lamb, the redeemed will be dressed in white.

They kept watch over their lives to live by the standards of God. Their reward is to be accepted at the wedding.

Revelation 3: 7 – 13 Philadelphia

Philadelphia is not a strong congregation, but that did not deter it from faithful service. For them there is neither rebuke nor warning. Christ is called Holy and true and seen holding the key of David. David was a man who loved God with all his heart. Maintaining that passionate love for God, which David had, is the key to their holding fast against opposition.

As in Smyrna, the opposition of the Jews is referred to as *the synagogue of Satan.* Despite not being a strong congregation they have persevered. God is mindful of their suffering and promises to keep them from further trials.

However it is possible to lose our crown if we allow ourselves to be misled. The Jews will try to drag them back under the law and in so doing close the door of salvation. They are encouraged to hold fast and not let these false teachers rob them of their crown. The *'name of my God'* states that from now on they will belong to God. They will also belong to the city of God the New Jerusalem and bear Jesus' new name of righteousness.

Revelation 3: 14 – 22 Laodicea

We come to a congregation which is smug, self-satisfied, wealthy, worldly wise and lacking enthusiasm for Christ. Yet Jesus still loves them and longs to have fellowship with them. The city of Laodicea was proud of its financial wealth, extensive textile industry and famous eye salve.

Comfortable with the world the congregation has ceased to be salt and light. In Leviticus, the Lord twice warned Israel, that if they became like the nations He was casting out, the land would likewise vomit them out (Leviticus 18: 25, 28, 20: 22). Jesus is repeating the same warning to His church. The prosperity, in which they take pride, emphasises their spiritual poverty. Real treasure comes from Jesus. We gain it through obedience to His word (Matthew 6: 19 – 24, Luke 12: 33).

Christ is called the *Amen, the Faithful and True Witness, the Beginning of Creation.* In this vision Jesus is calling them to look to the eternal kingdom not the passing wealth of this world.

Jesus does not call members out of the revolting smug Laodicean church. Instead He promises that if they stick it out, He will come to them. Their reward will be to share Christ's throne.

The one who cares

These letters reveal the personal relationship Jesus has with His body and His intimate knowledge of the circumstances within each congregation. We see His heart for the believers. He both encourages and rebukes. All through, the hardships and enticements of the world are presented as nothing compared to the blessings awaiting those who overcome.

REVELATIONS OF JESUS CHRIST

EL OLAM
ETERNAL GOD

Psalm 90: 2 proclaims that *"You had formed the earth and the world, even from everlasting to everlasting You are God."* This same theme of God being the everlasting Creator is taken up by the Elders in Revelation 4.

REFERENCE	TOPIC	TIMESPAN
Revelation 4: 1–11	**Christ The Eternal** A glimpse of the unchanging reality around the throne of God.	A scene which is outside time.

"Father, I desire that they also, whom You gave Me may be with Me where I am, that they may behold My glory which You have given Me; before the foundation of the world." John 17: 24

Why do we need to behold Christ's glory? We need to see Him enthroned in glory because it strengthens our faith. This vision of Christ helps us to understand how great He is. The angels know this already. They surround His throne in adoration and worship. But we in our earthbound vision tend to limit Him to a being just a little greater than ourselves. This vision corrects that myopia. Jesus is seated on His Father's throne surrounded in glory. By this we are assured that He *"...is able to do exceeding abundantly above all that we ask or think,..."* (Ephesians 3: 20).

In the centuries which have followed the receiving of this vision, the body of Christ has been through many dark times. There have been periods of intense persecution, when the whole world has seemed to be against the faithful. The intensity of persecution will increase towards the end of the age, *"for then there will be a great tribulation, such as has not occurred since the beginning of the world until now, nor ever shall be.*" Matthew 24: 21. In the storms of life and through the turbulence described in prophecy, the throne of God is where we anchor our faith. The world will pass away but the throne of God is eternal.

Therefore before the vision moves on to what lies ahead it focuses on the One who sits on the throne. We can have confidence that all which will happen in the future is in accordance with His plan.

Christ the Eternal

Revelation 4: 1 – 11

Revelation begins with the greeting, *'Grace and peace to you from Him who is, and who was, and who is to come, and from the seven spirits before His throne'*. (Revelation 1: 4). We are now transported into the presence of the One who sent that greeting. He is the Lord, the very centre of all creation. *'A door standing open,'* is in contrast to the closed door to the Laodicean Church. Mankind in sin leaves Jesus standing outside waiting to be invited in. Jesus through His sacrifice has opened the door to heaven to all who will go in.

Who is on the throne?

The first thing John sees is One sitting on a throne. The covenant delivered to Moses on Mount Sinai contains much which is intended to give us a picture of Heaven. To help us understand what is seen here, we need to refer to that covenant.

In Exodus 28: 15 – 21, there are instructions for making the High Priest's breastplate. On it are four rows of three stones, one for each of the tribes of Israel. The first stone of the first row is a Sardius. The last stone on the fourth row is a Jasper. Jesus is both the first and the last (Revelation 1: 17). The first stone is for the first son Reuben, whose name means 'behold a son'. The last stone on the fourth row is for Benjamin. His name means, 'son of my right hand'. The One sitting on the throne is like Jasper and Sardius. He is both *'behold a Son'* and *'Son of my right hand'*. Jesus alone carries both these titles.

The book of Hebrews tell us that Jesus, *"when He had by Himself purged our sins, sat down at the right hand of the majesty on high."* (Hebrews 1: 3). Sharing His Father's throne Jesus occupies His rightful place at the centre of heaven. He is the beloved Son who sits at the Father's right hand.

The Rainbow

The rainbow was given by God as a sign of His covenant (Genesis 9: 8 – 17). Some believe that the word translated *emerald* speaks of a crystal which dispersed light into many hues.

Four Living creatures

We will go next to the four living creatures and come back to the elders. Both *Isaiah* and *Ezekiel* were given visions of heaven. Isaiah sees the Lord sitting on His throne (Isaiah 6: 2 – 3). Above Him are seraphim. They are not described in detail, but like the creatures in Revelation each have six wings. Like the creatures in Revelation they cry *'Holy, Holy, Holy'*. Ezekiel in a vision also sees four living creatures (Ezekiel 1: 5 – 14). There is no doubt that these are the same creatures in each of the visions. The visions are so extraordinary that it is not surprising that the three prophets took in different aspects of these beings.

We are left with the question, what do these creatures represent? Fortunately the Bible is its own commentary. The camp of Israel was designed by God to convey an image of the order and pattern of heaven. Numbers 2: 1 – 3, 10, 18 and 25 sets out the organisation of the camp of Israel. The nation was grouped into four camps, each with three tribes. The tribes surround the tabernacle which represents the throne of God. Each of the four camps had its own banner. According to tradition Judah's banner was a lion, Reuben's banner a man, Ephraim's banner an ox and Dan's banner an eagle. They are the same as the four faces on each of the creatures described in Revelation.

After the victory over *Amalek*, *Moses* set up an altar to give glory for the victory to God (Exodus 17: 15). He gives the altar the name *YHWH Nissi* which means, *'The Lord is my banner.'* The banner represents covering and protection. Each of the banners of the camp represents one of the living creatures. By camping under the four banners the children of Israel were placing themselves under the covering of the four living creatures.

The living creatures are full of eyes and they do not rest day or night. I believe that they are angelic beings which constantly watch over the people of God. Their eyes see all that is going on in this world. They also gather up and return to God the prayers and praises of all His people.

The 24 Elders

In the layout of the camp the Levites were placed between the tribes and the tabernacle. They were divided into three family group camps, with Moses and Aaron and their families making up the fourth camp. (Numbers 3: 23, 29, 35, 38). The Levites surrounded the tabernacle and assisted in the worship of God.

Later when King David was preparing for the construction of the Temple, he divided the priests and Levites into divisions. The priests were divided into 24 divisions to serve (1 Chronicles 24: 1 – 19). The Levites were divided into 24 divisions to lead worship (1 Chronicles 25: 1 – 31). Each division in turn officiated at the service and worship in the Temple.

My personal understanding of the 24 elders seated around the throne picks up on this order, which I believe was inspired. In a similar way to the insight the Tabernacle gives into how we are to approach God, so I believe David was given prophetic insight into the ordered worship of Heaven. The Elders represent the heads of these divisions in heaven presiding over the worship of God.

In 1 Peter 2:9 we read that our eternal calling is to be a kingdom of priests to God. This is repeated in Revelation 1: 6 where Christ has made us kings and priests to His God. As in David's earthly kingdom, so in heaven, the worship of God will be orderly. The 24 Elders each lead their division of priestly worshippers. I believe that all the redeemed will be allocated to their respective division. In turn we will have the opportunity, on behalf of all the saved, to present our worship before the throne of God.

The Elders have crowns because they are kings as well as priests. They cast their crowns before the throne in recognition that all authority is in Christ. He is the creator and sustainer of all existence.

The Seven Spirits of God

Within the Tabernacle there was a candlestick, called the Menorah, with a central lamp and six branches (Exodus 25:31– 40, 37:17–24). The Menorah represents the seven spirits of God before His throne. That light was never to be allowed to go out. Earlier, Jesus refers to the seven lampstands as representing the seven churches. Here the seven lamps of fire before the throne are the seven spirits of God.

The connection between the seven lampstands representing the churches and the seven lamps which are the seven spirits of God, is simple. It is through the church that the Holy Spirit works in this world. If the church, as at Ephesus, has ceased to be a channel through which the Holy Spirit can work, the Lord will remove the lampstand (Revelation 2: 5).

The sea of glass like crystal and the emerald rainbow

The Tabernacle in its detailed order also provides a lesson on how we are to approach God.

At Mount Sinai the Lord invited *Moses, Aaron, Nadab* and *Abihu* with the seventy elders of Israel to climb the mountain and worship Him from afar. On the mountain they see the God of Israel. At His feet there was a pavement of Sapphire (Exodus 24: 10). Ezekiel likens his vision of the glory of the Lord to a rainbow (Ezekiel 1: 28). Emeralds and sapphires come in a range of colours blue through to green which may explain why John described the light as a rainbow. Exodus and Ezekiel both give us visions of the pre-incarnate Christ. Revelation now reveals Him restored to His former glory.

A bronze laver full of water was part of the furnishings of the Tabernacle (Exodus 30: 17 – 21).The Laver represented the sea of glass before the throne. It stood between the Altar for the burnt offerings and the entrance to the Tent of Meeting. Before entering the tent the priests had to wash their hands and feet. After our sins have been atoned for by sacrifice we still need to wash. Jesus referred to this when answering Peter's protest at having his feet washed (John 13: 6 – 10). Our sins were atoned for by Jesus on the cross, but in entering His presence we still need to ask for cleansing of the grime which we pick up in the world.

The sea of glass pure as crystal emphasises that nothing unclean can ever enter the presence of God. It is only through repentance and the blood of the Lamb that we can be cleansed from sin. The sea of glass may in some way reflect the expanse, sparkling like crystal that is referred to in Ezekiel 1: 22.

It's all about worship

Jesus is the One *'who was and is and is to come'*. He is the Lord God Almighty who lives forever and ever. He promises eternal life to all who believe in Him. Those closest to Jesus are filled with the most adoration and praise. They see Him for who He is and view with wonder the display of love in all His acts. He is worthy of praise because everything was made by Him. Nothing in heaven or earth exists without Him.

This vision of heaven reveals Christ in His eternal majesty. It has been given to encourage us before we move on to read of trouble to come. We have seen our Saviour on the throne and have the assurance that He has conquered death. In Him we will be victors and live for ever.

ELOHIM CHAYIN
THE LIVING GOD

At Sinai, the people in fear declared, *"For who is there of all flesh who has heard the voice of the living God .... as we have and lived?"* Deuteronomy 5: 26. Because Jesus died on our behalf and was raised to life we can all now enter the presence of the living God and live.

REFERENCE	TOPIC	TIMESPAN
Revelation 5: 1–14	We are given a glimpse of heaven on that glorious day when the Prince returns victorious from the mission which only He can accomplish.	Resurrection Day in heaven.

Mankind was created to look after God's creation. Through sin, man allowed Satan to take control. Jesus called Satan *"the ruler of this world."* (John 14: 30). In this revelation John weeps. He recognises that until someone is found who is worthy, no one can take back that rule from Satan. A perfect, sinless, obedient man has to be found. Satan mocks because, as the accuser, he knows that all of us have sinned. None is worthy.

Then Jesus is revealed, as the perfect sinless Lamb of God. Slain not because of His sin but in obedience to His Father. The One who willingly became a sacrifice for our sin, is worthy.

Christ who is worthy

Revelation 5: 1 - 14

Chapter 5 opens with the One on the throne holding a scroll. The significance of the scroll we are left to work out for ourselves. There are a number of things which we are told about it;

- It has writing on both the inside and outside.
- It has seven seals
- Only someone who was worthy could open it
- When no one was found worthy to open it John wept.
- When the Lamb takes the scroll the whole of heaven erupts in praise.
- As the scroll is opened it reveals conflict leading up to final victory.

John who received these visions had an advantage over us. He could read what was written on the outside. He immediately knew the content of the scroll. Held in the Father's right hand and sealed with seven seals conveys to us its importance. That importance is underlined by John weeping at the prospect of it remaining unopened.

As it is opened the story which unfolds is one of conflict. It is a conflict between two kingdoms. The kingdom of this world represented by four horsemen and the kingdom of heaven represented by the martyrs. It is an age long conflict lasting from the fall of mankind through to the establishment of the new heavens and new earth.

John then sees a strong angel, who I believe to be Satan, in his role of accuser. He cries out in a mocking voice, *"Who is worthy"*. While no one is found worthy, Satan remains the ruler of this world. [John 12:31].

The strong angel had come before the throne to claim that man, creation and all that is in it belonged to him and that he, Satan had won. He now discovers that the willing sacrifice of the Lamb of God upon the cross was not defeat, but victory.

He is worthy

This time it is an elder, not an angel, who speaks to John. An elder, because this matter concerns creation. *"Do not weep. Behold the Lion of the tribe of Judah, the Root of David, has prevailed to open the scroll and its seven seals."*

John is being taken back to events which took place many years before when he was a young man. He would remember watching as his Master was crucified. On that day all seemed lost. His hopes had come to nothing. He was there in the garden on resurrection day, coinciding with the festival of First Fruits, when defeat was turned into victory.

Sixty years on, John is allowed to see in a vision the scene in heaven on that day. He is allowed to witness the Lamb of God appearing triumphant before His Father's throne. The Lamb *"as though it had been slain."* has taken on Himself the penalty for our sin. The Father on the throne has found Him worthy and allows the Lamb to take the scroll from His hand.

In response the whole of heaven erupts in praise. The living creatures and the elders fall down in worship before the Lamb. The Elders, who represent mankind, cry out in praise, *"You were slain and have redeemed us to God by your blood."* Our victory and the victory of the kingdom of God is because of His victory. From that day on the redeemed and all of creation can, and one day will, give all the glory to the Father and the Son for ever and ever.

The Lamb

The Lamb is given the titles 'Lion of the tribe of Judah' and 'Root of David'. 'Lion of the tribe of Judah' alludes back to Genesis 49: 8 – 10, which is one of the first prophecies of the Messiah. Root of David alludes to Isaiah 11: 1 – 10, in which a branch shall come from the stem of Jesse. This passage in Isaiah is a wonderful prophecy of the triumphant Messiah. Having overcome Satan on the cross he is now able to claim the kingdom of the world for His own (Luke 19: 12). Seven horns represent all power and strength. Seven eyes describe One who sees everything and therefore has all knowledge and understanding.

The prayers of the saints

Throughout all of history there have been saints who have prayed for the coming of God's kingdom. These prayers are like incense to God (Psalm 141:2, Revelation 8:3) and have played their part in the victory now celebrated. The whole of creation and all the people of God will praise the Lamb for all He has done.

Worthy is the Lamb

First the living creatures and elders sing a new song. It is a song of praise for the completed work of Christ. It could not be sung prior to the atoning sacrifice of Christ. But now redemption has been accomplished. Salvation has come to every tribe, tongue, people and nation.

Next the angels take up the praise. Ten thousand times ten thousand is two hundred million. The vision hints that there are in fact many, many more. The angelic beings acknowledge that Jesus Christ, the Lamb is worthy of all power, riches, wisdom strength, honour, glory and blessing.

The whole of creation then erupts in songs of praise, which express the triumph of the cross. Jesus will reign forever and ever and we will share in His victory.

The victory has bought a people who will both serve in the worship of God, as priests, and also reign over His creation. (1 Corinthians 6:2-3, Titus 2:14). Paul wrote that when we are glorified by Jesus, the whole of creation will be set free (Romans 8: 18 – 23). Creation awaits eagerly the return of Christ to set it free from futility.

Satan mocked that no one was worthy. He was wrong.

The Lamb of God is worthy to take the scroll and reign.

There was a time when the Lamb laid down His life as atonement for our sin. Because of His faithfulness and obedience to His Father, He was raised from the dead as the First-Fruit of that greater eternal harvest. In heaven He now shares His Father's throne as the Living God.

EL RAKHUM

THE COMPASSIONATE GOD

When the Lord passed before Moses the first quality He announced was his compassion (mercy) (Exodus 34: 6). Our Lord is unchanged in His compassion for mankind.

REFERENCE	TOPIC	TIMESPAN
John 20: 11–18	The unchanging compassion of our Saviour.	Resurrection Day on earth.

Has being restored to glory changed Jesus? The following revelation of Christ may seem to be an aside but it reveals the unchanging character of our wonderful Saviour. Keep in mind the scene in heaven, as we ponder what happened down on earth two thousand years ago.

The Compassion of Christ

Mary Magdalene

The Holy Spirit led John to record in his gospel a scene which may seem to us to be just a quaint little aside. On this glorious resurrection day, standing just outside the empty tomb was a weeping and heartbroken young woman. She pours her heart out to one she thinks is the gardener. This story is the most beautiful testimony to the character of our Saviour. In the Psalms it is said that *"He heals the broken hearted and binds up their wounds"* (Psalm 147: 3). Here we find Jesus, in meeting Mary, doing precisely that. He comes to comfort her and help her take in the good news.

But note He goes on to say, *"Do not cling to me, for I have not yet ascended to my Father."* We go back to the vision of heaven. The Father on the throne, the living creatures, the elders and more that 200 million angels, are all waiting expectantly, on this the most glorious of all days.

They are waiting for the return of the conquering hero. What do we find Jesus doing? Taking time to comfort the broken hearted. Such is His love for those who love Him.

EL NEQAMAH
GOD OF VENGEANCE

After **King David** had been delivered from the hand of **Saul**, he wrote a psalm praising God. He proclaimed that it is God who avenges our enemies (2 Samuel 22: 48). The martyrs cry out *"how long until"* You judge. As David learned, God will judge but in His own time.

REFERENCE	TOPIC	TIMESPAN
Revelation 6: 1–17	An outline of the conflict between the kingdom of this world and the kingdom of God.	From creation to the New Heaven and New Earth.

God created a beautiful world for man to live in. It was an extension of the kingdom of heaven. Man sinned and fell under the domination of Satan, who jealously wanted this world for his own. There follows a war between the two kingdoms which at one time Satan nearly won. God found only one righteous family in the whole world. He saved that family but destroyed the rest in the Flood (Genesis 7: 23 - 24).

Man was given a new start. But soon Satan was at work again. He possessed a man, **Nimrod**, who established an empire and false religion (Genesis 10: 8 – 10). The centre of the kingdom was *Babel*, later called *Babylon*. God judged this kingdom at Babel by confusing the languages and causing men to spread out over the earth (Genesis 11: 1 – 11).

From out of that kingdom God chose a man, **Abraham**, to become a nation which would be His chosen people (Genesis 12: 1- 3). Later under Moses the chosen people were given the law, a way of worship and a land. Israel was to be the kingdom of God on earth, a blessing to all nations. In time Satan prevailed against Israel causing the nation to worship the false gods of the surrounding nations. God judged them by sending then into captivity in Assyria and Babylon.

After seventy years exile in Babylon they were partially restored to their land. Then after another four hundred years God sent His Son to proclaim the Kingdom and to offer Himself to the Jews as their King. They rejected Him; forty years later their city and temple were razed to the ground and the people scattered.

A new age opened in which the gospel was to be taken to every nation. Jesus said that before this present age ends *"this gospel will be preached in all the world as a witness to all nations..."* Matthew 24: 14. Rather than accept the rule of God, mankind will continue in its rebellion. When Jesus returns to claim His kingdom, the nations will gather to fight against Him. How will Jesus respond to this rebellion?

Christ the avenger
Revelation 6:1 – 17

Chapter 6 through to chapter 8 verse 1 cover the opening of the scroll. As each seal is opened the content of the scroll is revealed. The scroll summarises a conflict which has been in progress throughout history.

The seals

The first seal reveals a man who goes out to conquer. In Genesis chapter 10 we read of Nimrod. He was the first to go out to conquer and control men. After him many others have followed. They are deceived by Satan into coveting power and into the desire to 'lord it' over their fellow men. Some have recognised the Antichrist in the description of the rider. Nimrod was the first to seek to rule over others. The Antichrist when he comes will be the last in Nimrod's line.

*(As an aside, it is interesting to note that while Islam generally rejects the Bible, claiming that it has been corrupted, these verses are accepted. Both Sunni and Shiite see this as a reference to the coming Mahdi. Before his fall from power **Sadam Hussein** displayed many posters in Baghdad portraying himself as a medieval knight riding a white horse. He saw himself as the fulfilment of this prophecy.)*

The **second seal** reveals that the aftermath of conquest is not peace but war. The world's empires have never fulfilled the promise to bring peace and security. Satan presents his kingdom as the solution to the world's problems. The reality is always war.

The **third seal** describes famine, the inevitable consequence of war. The wheat and barley are sold at prices ordinary people cannot afford. Luxuries such as oil and wine, symbols of prosperity, are even further out of reach. In every conflict it is the poor who suffer most.

The **fourth seal** reveals that the end result of Satan's kingdom is death.

The history of the world can be summed up in the rise and fall of empires. The desire to conquer and control has always been followed by war, famine and death.

At the end of the age, the Antichrist will finally fulfil these prophecies. Despite his promise of peace, his reign will have the same outcome of war, famine and death.

The Martyrs

When **the fifth seal** is opened we see the other kingdom. It is not like the kingdom of this world. We have been warned that all who seek to serve God in this age will suffer (2 Timothy 3:12).

The history of the kingdom of God seems to be a story of defeat. The world is triumphant while the kingdom of God appears weak. The martyrs cry out for justice. Their faithfulness to Christ has brought them suffering. The original meaning of the word martyr covered more than the ones who gave up their lives. All who suffer in this life as faithful witnesses to Jesus are martyrs.

The martyrs are told to be patient. Victory is certain but they must wait until their number is complete. God will judge sinners in His own time (Luke 18: 7, 2 Thessalonians 1:6 - 10). The victorious each receives a white robe as has been promised the faithful in Sardis who have kept their robe from being soiled by the world (Revelation 3: 5). That robe is their wedding garment and assurance that they are clothed ready to enter the wedding feast (Revelation 19: 8).

The wrath of the Lamb

The overview of the conflict between the kingdoms ends with the wrath of the Lamb. Jesus spoke of the sun being darkened, the moon not giving its light and the stars falling from the sky, in reference to His coming and the day of judgement, following the reign of the Antichrist (Matthew 24: 29). The prophets also described the great and terrible day of the Lord in the same terms (Isaiah 2: 12 – 21, 13: 6 – 16, 24: 1 – 23, 34: 1 – 5, Joel 2: 31, 3: 14 – 16). As **the sixth seal** is opened, the people of the earth will wish that they could die rather than face the Lamb of God. There is no escape, not even death can protect, for all will be held to account before the throne of God.

The previous chapter reminded us of Jesus' compassion. He is long suffering, merciful, kind, patient and gentle. This chapter reveals another side of His character. There will come a day when His anger will terrify the people of this world. They mocked the faithful and tried to stamp out faith in Christ. He will avenge the suffering of His faithful servants. He will be the God of vengeance.

EL HANNE'EMAN
THE FAITHFUL GOD

"He is God, the faithful God". Deuteronomy 7: 9. Moses when addressing the nation of Israel assured them that God will keep the oath which He swore to their fathers because He is a faithful God. What was true then remains true today.

REFERENCE	TOPIC	TIMESPAN
Revelation 7: 1–8	God will be true to His promises toward Israel.	The final years of this age.
Revelation 14: 1–8	The faithful remnant.	

Has Jesus forsaken Israel?

There are many who believe that Israel no longer has a part in God's plan. It is widely taught that when the nation of Israel rejected Jesus, God rejected them and therefore the Christian church has replaced Israel in the purposes of God. According to this teaching the church is now the recipient of the promises previously made to that nation.

This revelation of Jesus Christ confirms that He still cares for Israel. He made a covenant with them, which He will not break. Romans 11: 29 assures us that *"the Gifts and calling of God are irrevocable."* God will not go back on His word.

Through the prophet *Amos*, God warned Israel that a time would come when He sifted the nation.

"For surely I will command, and will sift the house of Israel among all nations, as grain is sifted in a sieve; yet not the smallest grain will fall to the ground. All the sinners of my people shall die by the sword, who say 'The calamity shall not overtake nor confront us'." Amos 9: 9 – 10.

The faithful will be sieved but protected while the rebellious in the nation of Israel will not survive.

Christ the faithful

Revelation 7: 1 - 8

We now have a word for the people of Israel. Unbelieving Israel will suffer during the reign of the Antichrist and will be on earth when the wrath of God is poured out on the world. In Israel, God has a remnant who will turn to Christ at His coming (Zechariah 12: 10 – 14). Despite their present lack of faith in Christ they are sealed as a mark of His protection.

I believe that 144,000 is a symbolic number. It is divided into 12,000 from each tribe with the exception of Dan. Nothing more is said about them here other than they are sealed. They are sealed before any harm is done to the earth, sea and trees.

The numbering emphasises that God is watching over His people. Not one whom God has sealed will be lost. God knows them all. They will be part of His kingdom. He will protect them through these troubled times. In Ezekiel 9: 4 it is those who mourn over the sins of Israel who are sealed and protected. These are the remnant of Israel who are grieved by the nation's sin and rebellion. Although for a time blind to their Messiah, they will on that day, when He returns, come to faith in Him (Zechariah 12: 10). This prophecy is an assurance that not one who seeks to be faithful to God, despite not knowing Christ, will be lost.

The tribe of Dan is missing from the list of tribes to emphasise that this is still a salvation by faith. Dan was the only tribe who failed to have the faith to claim their inheritance in the Promised Land (Judges 18:1). Instead they occupied the inheritance of another. Their exclusion from the list is a reminder that not all Israel by natural descent will sit down at the wedding feast (Luke 13: 18). Salvation for both Jew and Gentile is through faith in Christ. Without faith the Jew, as with the Gentile, will perish.

It is also a warning to the Gentile that we cannot enter the Kingdom of Heaven by living in someone else's inheritance. Our parents or grandparents may have had faith but that will not save us. Only by making that faith our own, can we enter into the wedding feast (John 3: 16, Matthew 25: 1 – 13).

Revelation 14: 1 - 5

Revelation Chapter 13 describes Satan's last desperate attempt to reassert his authority in this world. His man, the beast, seeks to lead the whole world astray. Despite all Satan's efforts, the reign of the beast ends in defeat. There is a glorious conclusion to that time of tribulation brought about by Satan. When the Lamb of God returns to defeat the beast and overthrow Satan's kingdom, a remnant from the people of Israel will repent and receive Him as their Messiah.

It is a sound principle of interpretation that once we have determined the meaning of a symbol, within a book of the Bible, we do not change that meaning when the symbol is repeated later in the book. Therefore it is the same 144,000, as described in Revelation 7: 1 – 8, who are now seen praising God. None of those whom God has sealed will be lost. In contrast to the mark, name and number of the beast, the 144,000 all bear the name of the Father on their foreheads. They now belong to Him. They refused the mark of the beast. For that reason they are counted as pure.

They are seen standing on Mount Zion which is the place from which our Lord will reign (Isaiah 2: 3). This emphasises their particular connection with that city and the land. As their protector, Jesus will bring these 'sealed' through the final time of trial. Out of rebellious Israel a new nation is born. They are called first fruits because Israel was chosen first. The full harvest of the Gentiles is seen a little later in the prophecy.

A literal translation of verse 2 reads, *"And I hear sound out of heaven as sound of many waters and as sound of loud thunder, and the sound which I hear as lyre singers playing on their harps."* This helps us to understand that the thunderous sound coming out of heaven is the praises of the redeemed out of Israel. It is a new song because at last their eyes have been opened to recognise their Messiah. No one else can learn the song for it springs from that special and unique relationship which Israel has with God. It is between them and the Lord Jesus.

Redeemed and sanctified they faithfully follow the Lamb. Having now repented and put their faith and trust in Jesus they are considered without fault. There is no longer any deceit in their mouths because God has given them a new heart and put His Spirit within them (Ezekiel 36: 24 – 28). They are said not to be defiled with women. The Lord warned Israel, through Hosea and the other prophets, that following other gods was in His eyes adultery. The enticements of the beast did not trap them. Therefore they are described as virgins.

A nation born in a day

The reign of the beast will be a time of separation. It is the plan of God to use it to call out the few who stand faithful to Him, from the many who will be deceived (2 Thessalonians 2: 11 – 12). In Romans we read that a time will come when the full number of Gentiles has come in (Romans 11: 25). That number will be completed during the final three and a half years of the beast's reign. Once the number of the Gentiles is complete, *"a deliverer will come out of Zion, and He will turn away ungodliness from Jacob."* Romans 11: 26. According to Zechariah, it will be on the day that the Lord comes to the defence of Israel that they will recognise their Messiah. On that day, the remnant of the nation which has been protected and preserved during the time of trouble will repent. *"And at that time your people shall be delivered, everyone who is found written in the book."* Daniel 12: 1

Jesus Christ is always faithful to His word.

Will the Jews suffer even more?

This is a question which exercises many. Some teach that their suffering is past. All that now lies ahead is the conversion of Israel as they come to recognise their Saviour. Those who love Israel must truly hope that these people are right. However there are a number of scriptural prophecies which point to one last end time period of suffering. One of these is John 5:43 which I believe is prophetic. The reason Israel will have one last terrible period of suffering is because, having rejected their Messiah, they will now look to the one who comes in his own name, a reference to the Antichrist.

Israel will be saved

Unwittingly Israel will let herself in for a terrible time of suffering. When all hope is lost they will be forced to cry out to the Lord for help. In the end, because God has made promises to Israel which He cannot break, the nation will repent and accept Jesus as their king. Because He is faithful, He will at that time rescue them.

REVELATIONS OF JESUS CHRIST

YESHUA
SALVATION

"And He has become my salvation". Exodus 15: 2. God freed Israel from slavery in Egypt. He cast their enemies into the sea. We have been set free from the slavery of sin by One who bears the name *Salvation*.

REFERENCE	TOPIC	TIMESPAN
Revelation 7: 9 – 8:1 **Revelation 15: 1–4**	The triumph of the kingdom of Heaven.	The beginning of the millennial reign of Christ.

Why did Jesus come into this world? Was it as a great teacher who would give moral guidance to make the world a better place? Was it to set an example of sacrificial love to inspire us to love our neighbours? We learn in this revelation that Jesus had something else in mind. He came seeking a bride. He calls out of this present rebellious, sinful world a people who will love and trust Him. This is a revelation which we can only understand if first we have recognised how far short we have fallen from obedience to God.

Christ the Saviour

Revelation 7: 9 – 8: 1

At the beginning of this vision John wept, because no one could open the scroll. He thought that the battle had been lost and Satan was victorious. Then he sees the Lamb as though He had been slain. Jesus Christ returns from earth to heaven as the victor. The Father accepts His beloved Son, who was perfect in obedience, as the One who is worthy.

Now John sees the fruit of the victory, a great multitude from every tribe and nation. The multitude has come out of the great tribulation, which in the context of this passage refers to the whole time in which the battle between the two kingdoms has raged. The world hates the

Kingdom of God. It hates Jesus, in the same way it hates His followers (John 15: 18 – 25, 2 Timothy 3: 12).

The palm branches in the hands of the great crowd would, to the Jew, have symbolized the Feast of Tabernacles, (Leviticus 23: 39 – 43), which is a celebration of the Harvest. We now see the fruit of that harvest. The repentant nation of Israel is joined by Gentiles from every tribe and nation. The distinction between Jew and Gentile has been removed. We are now all one in Christ.

'Tabernacles' is also widely understood to represent the 1000 year reign of Christ on earth. As the ingathering of harvest it prefigures the gathering of Jews and Gentiles during the Messiah's reign (Isaiah 27: 12 – 13, Zechariah 14: 16 – 17).

The multitude, which cannot be numbered, are dressed in fine linen. At the end of Revelation we discover that the people dressed in fine linen are also the bride of Christ (Revelation 19: 7 – 8). Besides a harvest festival, this is also a wedding celebration.

The multitude cry out with one voice, *"Salvation belongs to our God who sits on the throne, and to the Lamb."* To be part of this great gathering, the first step is to recognize the need of a Saviour.

Sinners needing grace

It is easy to think of ourselves as only needing a little improvement. We justify our failings pretending that they are not serious. We need first to recognize that *"all have sinned and fallen short of the glory of God"* Romans 3: 23. The prophet Isaiah wrote that sin creates a barrier between us and God. *"But your iniquities have separated you from God; and your sins have hidden His face from you."* Isaiah 59: 2.

It is only when we realize that we are in danger that we cry out to be rescued. The danger we face is described at the end of Revelation. All who remain in rebellion and unrepentance will be cast into the lake of fire. None need end up in that terrible place. There is a Saviour who can rescue us, His name is Jesus.

The angels, elders and living creatures all worship God. There will be eternal praise for the wisdom of God, in that He found a way to rescue us from our sin.

The blood of the Lamb

The whole vast multitude, from every tribe and nation, have one thing in common. They have *"washed their robes and made them white in the blood of the Lamb"*. Repeatedly in the Old Testament we are reminded that the blood of an animal must not be eaten. The blood represents the creature's life (Leviticus 17: 11). Jesus, in shedding His blood, gave His life for us. It is not called the blood of Jesus but the blood of the Lamb. This is to remind us that Jesus became a willing sacrifice, to atone for our sins. When John the Baptist pointed to Jesus, he said, *"Behold the Lamb of God, which taketh away the sin of the world."* John 1: 29. Our Lord Jesus has taken on the punishment for our sin by His death.

A hint of heaven

We now have a first hint of what will be expanded on at the end of Revelation. God will dwell among men and we will serve Him. The 24 elders will be in charge of the praise which will continue unbroken day and night. There will be no more hunger, no more thirst, no more unbearable sun or heat, and no more tears. Our Saviour the Lamb will lead and look after his people.

The Seventh Seal

The silence is the peace following war. The conflict between the two kingdoms is ended. People have been redeemed out of every tribe and nation. There will be a new Heaven and a new Earth, which will enjoy peace forever and ever (Revelation 21 & 22).

Jesus came into this world to redeem a people and prepare a bride for Himself. He became our Saviour bearing the punishment for our sin. This present world and all that is in it will one day be destroyed, (2 Peter 3: 10). Jesus is saving people out of this world that they may enter His new heaven and new earth.

In this chapter we have seen that there is a vast harvest out of all the Gentile nations. A harvest that has been reaped throughout history. We come now to another harvest.

Revelation 15: 1 – 4

This is the wheat harvest, which Jesus reaps, at the very end of the age (Matthew 13: 24 – 31). Of this harvest it is said that they are, *"those who have the victory over the beast, over his image, and over the number of His name."* This last group are those who have persevered during the reign of the beast. They have heeded the warnings in Revelation that it will be a time when many will be killed or imprisoned for their faith. Having been prepared they stood firm and overcame the deceptions of the enemy.

In Daniel 7: 25 we read of the beast *"He shall speak pompous words against the Most High, shall persecute the saints of the Most High and shall intend to change the times and law. Then the saints shall be given into his hand for time, times and half a time."* God will allow this persecution for His purposes.

Later, we will discover that this group who remain faithful will receive special responsibilities and privileges in Christ's kingdom. But those who give in and receive the mark of the beast will receive terrible punishment.

This group is standing on the sea of glass close to the presence of God. Like the 24 Elders they have harps of gold. I believe that is because their praise, born out of endurance, is especially precious to God. The song is that of the two great leaders who set the people of God free. Moses brought the people out of slavery in Egypt. The Lamb sets us free from slavery to the kingdom of this world. The joy over deliverance from slavery in Egypt becomes joy at deliverance from the world.

When we stand before His presence, after the battles of this life are over, the joy will be ours, the glory will all be His.

"Great and marvellous are your works, Lord God Almighty
Just and true are your ways, O King of the saints.
Who shall not fear you, O Lord, and glorify Your name?
For You alone are holy.
For all nations shall come and worship before You,
For Your judgments have been manifest."

REVELATIONS OF JESUS CHRIST

ADONAI YAHWEH
LORD GOD

After the defeat at Ai, *Joshua* cried out to the Lord, why had He brought them so far only to be destroyed (Joshua 7: 7). For a moment Joshua gave up hope. The Lord responded with the challenge to be obedient and trust Him. When dark times come we must recognise that the Lord God is sovereign and in control.

REFERENCE	TOPIC	TIMESPAN
Revelation 8: 2 **to** **Revelation 9: 21**	The conflict which rages in the heavenly realm. All the judgements have an angelic component.	The closing period of the Church Age.

So far Revelation has laid a foundation of the character and purpose of Christ. We now move on to the turmoil which has been caused by Satan's rebellion. We have been warned.

The Bible is a prophetic book. Nearly one in three verses looks forward to events which were still future at the time of writing. Predictive prophecy is the seal on the Bible's inspiration. It lifts scripture from being the words of man to the assurance that we are studying the word of God.

Biblical prophecy is not the outcome of the Lord's greater intelligence, an intelligence which enables Him to make more accurate predictions of future events than we can. Nor is it the result of His foreknowledge which enables Him to reveal the future. The Lord states in Isaiah, *"And new things I declare; before they spring forth I tell you of them."* Isaiah 42: 9. Our God speaks the future into existence. He both determines and declares what will happen.

Our God is Sovereign and yet at times He can seem far distant. It is as if He has turned His back on the world. In our studies of the revelations of Jesus Christ from the book of Revelation, we come to a section in which we might well ask, where is Christ in all of this?

As the seals of the scroll are opened, a conflict is revealed. It is the struggle on earth between two kingdoms. The kingdom of this world, intent on conquest, and the kingdom of heaven. The kingdom of the world brings war, famine and death. During this time, the martyrs, who represent the kingdom of God, are told to be patient. The vision moves on, from the conflict on earth, into the spiritual realm.

Christ the Sovereign

Revelation 8: 2 – 9:21

Looking ahead to chapter 12, we read that there is war raging in heaven. That war ends when Satan is defeated and thrown down to earth. I believe that in this section the sounding of trumpets declare preceding victories in heaven. As a result demonic forces are cast down to the earth to wreak their havoc here. The trumpets sound as a celebration of victory and also a warning to the earth.

The prayers of the saints

When the fifth seal was opened, we heard the prayers of the martyrs, *"How long, Sovereign Lord, holy and true, until you judge the inhabitants of the earth and avenge our blood."* These prayers and all our prayers, combined with incense, ascend before the throne. What follows is the response to these prayers.

We enter a period of judgment on the earth. Each of the first six judgments contain an element of fire. Fire is also a symbol of angels: *"He makes his angels winds, His servant's flames of fire."* Hebrews 1: 7.

War in heaven

In heaven warfare is being waged. The first four trumpets announce victories being won in heaven. Demonic forces are cast down to earth to wreak their own forms of havoc. We do not see the demons, but the effect of their actions are all around us. They spur men on to disobey God.

The trumpets

With the first four trumpets it is the environment which suffers. First trees and grasslands are destroyed. Then the seas are polluted so that the fish die and ships are sunk. Water sources become undrinkable and sunlight is reduced.

Over thirty years ago, when my father started the quarterly prophecy newsletter *Trumpet Sounds*, it was in the belief that these trumpets were already sounding. The 20th century saw unprecedented war, famine, death and destruction. The global environment has come under threat causing people to fear for the future of the planet.

In the last century deforestation took place on an enormous scale. Through the extremes caused by a changing climate and over grazing, grasslands have turned to desert. Diseases have wiped out whole species of trees. In the wars of the 20th century a vast tonnage of shipping was sunk. The seas have become polluted by waste chemicals and plastics. Fish stocks are depleted to the point where many species are near to extinction.

There has been widespread pollution of water sources. A large proportion of the world's population does not have access to clean drinking water. Drinking from these polluted sources brings the risk of disease. Wormwood is a plant with a strong bitter taste.

Burning rainforests in the Far East have blotted out the sun. Air pollution is a problem in many industrialised countries. Over the final three decades of the 20th century the intensity of sunlight reaching the surface of the earth has reduced. In places the reduction has been measured as thirty percent.

These judgements will intensify as we near the end of the age. As with the judgments which fell on Egypt, at the time of Moses, it is the natural world which is first to suffer. God will allow the demons to use the forces of nature to bring destruction. The demonic forces will also stir man to wage war and cause destruction due to greed. Trees, grass, rivers, lakes, the sea and the atmosphere, are all part of our common heritage and responsibility. The present environmental crisis is a warning of greater judgments to come.

The three woes

The final trumpets announce times of great distress. Demons are released to torment men, causing them to seek death. Men become the target of the attack. The grass, plants and trees are protected.

When Satan is thrown out, there is a great celebration in heaven. But for the earth it will be a time of woe (Revelation 12: 12). In this passage the star fallen from heaven is Satan. On being cast out of heaven Satan is given permission to open the bottomless pit and release those who are imprisoned there.

The bottomless pit is a terrible place, even demons fear it. When Jesus cast the demons out of *Legion* they pleaded with Him not to send them there (Luke 8:31). In sending the demons elsewhere Jesus demonstrated that He has power over who goes into that place.

Evil angels were responsible for the degenerate state of man and the world, in the days of *Noah*. God imprisoned the fallen angels keeping them in bonds until the Day of Judgment (2 Peter 2: 4, Jude 6). For a short time they will be released from the pit to paralyse people with fear (Revelation 9: 2 - 6).

The first woe

The torment of mankind is permitted in order to bring about repentance. Those who have the seal of God on their foreheads are protected. Ezekiel received a vision just before the fall of Jerusalem. He saw the angel of the Lord go through the city, putting a mark on the foreheads of the godly, who grieve over the sin of the nation (Ezekiel 9: 4). The angel is followed by the executioners. They slay without mercy all who do not have the mark, beginning with the ungodly Elders in the Temple. All who trust in God will not fear, being confident that they are in His safe keeping.

The demons are not visible but their torture will be very real. The vivid description emphasises the power of their attack. War horses are creatures without fear. Crowns symbolise authority. Faces of men represent intelligence. Women's hair indicates effeminacy. Lion's teeth warn that the attack will be ferocious. Iron breast plates covering their hearts signifies that they will have no mercy. Wings will enable this evil to spread rapidly over the whole earth. Stings of scorpions torture rather than kill. In mercy, God who is sovereign will limit the duration of this plague.

The king over them

"They have over them a king, the angel of the abyss, whose name in Hebrew is 'Abaddon' and in Greek his name is 'Apollyon'." Most conventional interpretations pay no further attention to Abaddon. It seems that he is released to disappear. This interpretation sets out that he is the principal character in all that follows.

His names mean *'destruction'* or *'destroyer'*, which are both terms used in scripture for the Antichrist. Isaiah refers to the one who will oppress the land as the destroyer (Isaiah 14 and 15), prior to a throne being established in mercy and truth (Isaiah 16: 5). Paul refers to the Antichrist as *the son of perdition* or destruction (2 Thessalonians 2: 3). This king, of the abyss, who has been imprisoned for centuries ready for this hour, will from now on, in Revelation, be referred to as the beast.

The second woe

This woe will be the most awful time in the history of man, to be compared with the days of the flood.

In the vision of the seals the four winds are restrained until the servants of God are sealed (Revelation 7: 3). Word is now given that the evil angels are to be restrained no longer. These four evil angels stir the whole world to war. The horses and their riders are the unseen demonic forces that drive men on to fight and destroy each other.

The outcome of this devastating conflict will be the rise of the last great World Empire, the empire of the Beast. This war is the worst, which will ever take place on the earth. Many will refer to it as *Armageddon,* which it is not. Armageddon takes place *after* the reign of the beast.

John who receives this vision is staggered by the numbers involved. He emphasises that he heard the number, which is two hundred million. This was in a day when the population of the entire Roman Empire was about seventy million. The result of this war is the death of one third of mankind.

God does not want to punish men. He seeks their repentance from which can come restoration to His love (2 Peter3: 9). But men will refuse Him preferring their wickedness to submission to God.

Six sins are listed against man, the worship of demons, the worship of idols, murder, sorcery (literally: enchantment with drugs), sexual immorality and theft. It is a description of man without moral restraint.

It has been said that the sins of man ultimately lead to the ''*man of sin*'. Due to refusing to repent of their sins, men will be given over to Satan for the last tragic period of world history. The kingdom of the beast which follows is the second part of this woe.

Where is Jesus?

In the midst of all this conflict and deception we may ask, where is Christ in this? In Revelation 9: 1, the fallen star is Satan. The verse goes on, *"To him was given the key to the bottomless pit."* Who holds the key to the pit? According to Revelation 1:18 Jesus has the keys of death and hades which includes the pit. Jesus is sovereign. The demonic powers held in the pit can only be released when Jesus decides that the time has come.

An alternative translation of 2 Thessalonians 2: 6, 7 which I prefer reads as follows; *"And now you know the holding back, for him to be revealed in his time. For the mystery of lawlessness already is working, only He is restraining now, until he comes out of the midst."* J P Green's literal translation.

Instead of the restrainer being taken out of the way, 2 Thessalonians speaks of One who is restraining, until the time comes for the man of sin to be revealed. It is Jesus the Christ who restrains. In all the turbulence of these times, Jesus is revealed as being firmly in control. Satan, even in his bid to rule the world, is restrained by Christ.

Jesus Christ is in all things both Lord and Sovereign.

REVELATIONS OF JESUS CHRIST

LUCIFER
THE ANTICHRIST

Lucifer is the Latin name for *the morning star* and may be translated as *bearer of light*. The King James Version of Isaiah 14: 12 reads, **"How are you fallen from heaven, O Lucifer, son of the morning!"** This angel will appear to be the bringer of light and peace but his reign will be evil.

REFERENCE	TOPIC	TIMESPAN
Revelation 10: 1–10	Following a period of conflict there will be a great deception. We must not be deceived.	The closing period of the Church Age.

"For false christs and false prophets will rise and show great signs and wonders to deceive if possible even the elect." Matthew 24: 24. Can the elect be deceived? Jesus insisted that we must remain vigilant and not believe those who falsely claim that Jesus has returned (Matthew 24: 26). Therefore the answer would appear to be, yes, they can be deceived, if they do not watch.

At the end of the age there will be a final deceiver. In the Bible he is given several titles; *the antichrist, the man of sin, the little horn, the beast* and *the lawless one*. The apostle Paul writes, *"the coming of the lawless one is according to the working of Satan, with all power, signs and lying wonders, and with all unrighteous deception among those who perish,......"* 2 Thessalonians 2: 9 – 10.

Christ and the great deception
Revelation 10: 1 - 10

Chapter 10 introduces us to a mighty angel. Who is he? Is this a picture of Christ or another holy angel sent to bring further revelation to John? Personally I don't think that he is either of these. Although this angel is magnificent in appearance he is not Christ.

He appears to have the attributes of Christ. He comes with the cloud, which in many places in scripture symbolises the Lord's presence (Exodus 24:16). The rainbow symbolises the covenant with man (Genesis 9: 16). In the first section of Revelation, Jesus is described as having feet like bronze glowing in the furnace, similar to the statement here that his feet were as pillars of fire. This mighty angel cried with a loud voice as a lion roars. *Isaiah, Jeremiah* and *Joel* each speak of the Lord roaring when He comes to mount Zion to fight for Israel. This description could suggest that it is a vision of our Lord at the time of His return. But if it is the second coming, why is the vision inserted here, interrupting the sequence of the prophecy?

Following His incarnation, Jesus is never referred to as 'an angel'. He used the title '*Son of Man*' for Himself. His identity both in Heaven and on earth is now the '*Son of Man*' (Matthew 26:24, Daniel 7:13, Revelation 1:13). In the introduction to Revelation, John recognises One like the Son of Man. The fact that John does not recognise this mighty angel as the Son of Man questions this being a vision of Jesus.

An alternative interpretation could be that this is *Michael* the Archangel. His name means '*who is like God*'. Therefore to have a likeness to God is not unexpected. In Daniel 12: 1, Michael stands up to defend Israel in their time of trouble. In Revelation, Michael is the one who leads the fight against Satan. However I do not believe that this angel is Michael.

The great deception

Another interpretation, which I believe to be correct, is that this is not Christ at all, but one who comes imitating Him. A person who says of himself, *"I will ascend into heaven; I will exalt my throne above the stars of God, I will also sit on the mountain of the congregation on the farthest sides of the north; I will ascend above the heights of the clouds; I will be like the Most High."* Isaiah 14: 13, 14.

He is the one who wishes to appear to the world as God. *"the son of destruction, who opposes and exalts himself above every so-called god or object of worship, so that he takes his seat in the temple of God, displaying himself as being God."* 2 Thessalonians 2: 4.

This interpretation fits the flow of the prophecy. It brings Antichrist into this world between the release of Abaddon and the beast being active in slaying the two witnesses.

Satan's mighty angel

I believe that this is the same mighty angel, the accuser, who mocked because no one was found worthy to open the seals. It is Satan, permitted by God, to work his great deception on the world. Satan, unlike Jesus, cannot become incarnate as a man. Jesus out of love for us became one of us, so that He could take on Himself the penalty for our sin. Satan hates mankind and seeks to destroy us. Even if he could become man, his pride and hate would prevent his doing so. Instead he will take over and possess a man who has been preserved for this purpose. This man is the beast from the abyss.

Satan, defeated in Heaven, will masquerade through this man, as an angel of light (2 Corinthians 11: 14). He will deceive the world into believing that the real Christ has come. If this interpretation is correct it emphasises the magnitude of the deception which Satan will be allowed to perpetrate on the world.

Jesus was received into heaven in a cloud. The angels told the disciples that He would return in the same way as they saw Him go (Acts 1: 9 - 11). Satan now comes clothed in a cloud, in the pretense of fulfilling prophecy. Muslims believe that their Jesus will descend from the clouds to join the Mahdi for the final battle.

Jesus when He comes to fight for Israel will roar like a lion. But the beast also has the mouth of a lion (Revelation 13:2) and Satan *"prowls about like a roaring lion"* 1 Peter 5: 8. He will roar like a lion in imitation of Christ. The mighty angel has a rainbow as a sign of the covenant.

The Antichrist will make a covenant with Israel, but it will be a covenant of Death (Isaiah 28: 15).

The seven thunders are Satan's imitation of the seven spirits of God. The Spirit of God leads us into all truth. The thunders speak lies. That is why John is not allowed to record what they said.

The angel's arrival follows the catastrophic war. He comes as the one the world has been longing for. He is seen as a peacemaker, who will solve all the problems of the world. The angel takes up his position on the sea shore, from where the beast arises.

At the beginning of the vision of the seals, we saw Christ claiming the scroll, much to the delight of John. This angel only has a little scroll. It is poor counterfeit of the scroll that would have entitled him to rule this world, but which through the sacrifice of Jesus he was denied.

When John takes and eats the scroll, which the angel holds, it is sweet to his mouth but bitter in his stomach. *Ezekiel* was given, by God, a scroll to eat (Ezekiel 3:1 - 3). Although it contained bitter words against Israel, it was sweet to the mouth. When God rebukes and chastises us, it is sweet because it is done in love. This little scroll however, appears at first to be the word of God, but its effect is bitter. Psalm 55: 20 – 21, speaks of a betrayer whose *"mouth was smoother than butter, but his heart was war; his words were softer than oil, yet they were drawn swords"*. The words on the scroll are treachery to the whole world.

In this interpretation it is the voice from heaven, not the angel, which tells John to take the scroll. John, having tasted the scroll, understands the bitter outcome of Satan's rule. He is commanded to warn the world of the consequence of accepting Satan's reign. The prophecies which follow contain that warning.

Does this angel speak the truth?

The angel declares that when the seventh angel is about to sound the mystery of God will be finished. Is that true? No, it is the seventh trumpet which announces the establishment of the kingdom of God

(Revelation 11: 15). Satan seeks to pre-empt this by declaring that the kingdom has come. Having been cast out of heaven, Satan knows that he has only a short time left (Revelation 12: 12). This vision describes Satan's strategy for blocking the completion of God's work. With only a little time left, he offers the world his own 'christ'. In his blasphemy he will pretend that it is all in accordance with prophecy. The ignorant will be taken in.

With all power, signs and lying wonders

How powerful is Satan? I do not know. But I believe that he will be able to put on a convincing show. In the revealing of the man of sin, every aspect of the return of Christ will, as far as Satan is able, be counterfeited. There will be signs and lying wonders designed to shake the faith of Christians. Remember, the primary purpose of this deception is to fool Christians. The rest of the world has been deceived already.

This passage reveals the enormity of the deception that Satan plans to perpetrate on this world, by displaying his proxy as Christ. The angel's arrival follows the catastrophic war. He comes as the peace maker the world longs for and claims to be the one who can solve all the problems of the world.

Although this is a book about revelations of Jesus Christ in the book of Revelation, we need to pause here and ponder. This imitation 'christ' will bring great confusion to many Christians, especially to those who have a sketchy knowledge of prophecy. To those who have only a limited understanding, prophecy will appear to be fulfilled by this man of sin. Yet, for those who know their Bible there will be things which do not ring true.

There is one great distinction between the coming of Christ and the appearing of the Antichrist. When the Antichrist appears he will be welcomed by the World. When Jesus returns He will fill people with terror (Revelation 6: 15 – 17).

Be not deceived

Jesus warned of the danger of being deceived, *'So as to mislead, if possible, even the elect'* (Mark 13: 22 and Matthew 24: 24). Most Christians file this away at the back of their minds, complacent in the belief that it could not happen to them. We repeat, Satan's prime intention with the presentation of his 'messiah' is to deceive the elect. Everyone else he has already deceived through false religions, philosophies or material wellbeing. There is one group he must also bring into his kingdom, those who hold to the testimony of Jesus.

Woe to those who believe that prophecy is a subject that need not concern them. They are at risk of being deceived in this final hour of tribulation. This imitation 'christ' will bring great confusion to many Christians. Much of prophecy will appear to be fulfilled in him. We need to know our Lord and His Word, so that we are able to stand in the evil day and not be deceived. He has warned us beforehand.

EL HANNORA

THE AWESOME GOD

In a time of distress *Nehemiah* called on the great and awesome God, who keeps His covenant of mercy with those who love Him (Nehemiah 1: 5). Likewise *Daniel* brought his intercession for the nation to the great and awesome God (Daniel 9: 4). Awesome in the sense that He is the one to be feared. In the troubled times that will close this age we are to remember that we trust a great and awesome God. He is merciful but also to be feared for He will judge the world in righteousness.

REFERENCE	TOPIC	TIMESPAN
Revelation 10: 11 to Revelation 11: 18	God will not leave Himself without a witness.	The closing period of the Church Age.

We come to the closing years of this age when the Antichrist, here called the beast, will be allowed to reign. His reign is the second part of the second woe; the first part being the war which brings the beast to power. The third woe, which closes this section, is the announcement of the kingdom of our Lord and of His Christ. The establishment of Christ's kingdom is a woe for the sinful and rebellious. They know that they will now suffer His wrath.

The kingdom of the beast is described later in Revelation. In this passage we read of God's first priority, which is the true believers. It also reveals that Jesus will never leave himself without a witness in this world. Satan deceives the world with displays of supernatural power. God in mercy sends two witnesses who are given power to counter Satan's deception and warn of coming wrath.

Christ and His witnesses

Revelation 10: 11 – 11:18

The Greek word *'Naos'* is translated here as *'Temple.'* It can designate the Temple building proper, as distinct from the outer courts. The word is also used in the New Testament to refer to the church (Ephesians 2: 21).

Gentiles, considered unbelievers, were permitted to enter the outer courts of the Temple, but access to the inner courts was forbidden. John is told to rise and measure the temple of God, the altar and the people there. The outer court was not to be measured as the Gentiles will trample it forty two months.

Zechariah had a vision of a man measuring Jerusalem, which symbolised her divine protection (Zechariah 2: 1 – 5). The command to measure the temple of God, the altar and the people, speaks of God's protection of the faithful. This vision is an assurance that, during the time which lies ahead, true believers are under the protection of God.

They will not be subjected to any greater suffering than they will be given strength to bear.

The witnesses

The outer court refers to the false church and unfaithful Israel who will suffer outside the protection of God. The Antichrist will set his throne in Jerusalem and reign for forty two months or three and a half years. During this time God will not be without a witness. He sends two men who have been prepared for this hour. They are clothed in sackcloth as a sign of God's mourning over a sinful world which is heading for an outpouring of His wrath.

Zechariah saw a vision of a lampstand with seven lights on it and two olive trees beside it. When he asks the angel what the meaning of the olive trees is, he is told *"These are the two who are anointed to serve the Lord of all the earth"* Zechariah 4: 11 - 14. These witnesses have been specially prepared and anointed for this time that the power of God may flow through them.

On the Mount of Olives, our Lord spoke about the events that will lead up to His return. He spoke of a time when His followers will be hated and persecuted by all nations. Many will fall away, others will be misled by false prophets. But despite the apostasy it appears that it is during this final time of persecution, that the church will complete its commission to take the gospel to all nations (Matthew 24: 9–14). We will not be able to witness openly. It is when we are hauled before the courts that our witness will be proclaimed. We are not to worry about what to say, the Lord will speak through us (Luke 21: 12 - 19).

The two witnesses will be able to speak openly, for the Antichrist will be forbidden to harm them. They will stand, like *Elijah* in his day, against the wickedness that is in the world (1 Kings 17 & 18, James 5: 17) and will be granted the same authority as exercised by Moses to bring plagues on the earth (Exodus 7 to 12). The church will also witness by standing firm in the face of persecution. By this means in this last hour the whole world will hear the gospel. Speaking about standing steadfast in the face of persecution Jesus said, *"By your patience possess your souls"*. Luke 21: 19. The call to stand firm is repeated over and over by our Lord. He will be our Strength.

The death of the witnesses

When the beast slays the witnesses the world will rejoice. At last they are rid of all that disturbs their conscience. The witnesses are dead and the Christians have been silenced, so that none dare openly condemn the world for its actions. The celebrations will be short lived. When the witnesses are raptured (v.12) the world will realise that the words they spoke are true. In celebrating their death the people of the world have condemned themselves by their actions.

Even at this time if a person repents he can be saved. *'And everyone who calls on the name of the LORD will be saved;'* Joel 2: 32, referring to the great and terrible day of the Lord which follows the rapture of the church.

Note: the distinguishing identity of the beast both here and later, is his coming from the abyss (Revelation 11:7, 17:8). Abaddon is the only one who is identified as arising from the pit. Later we will receive the extraordinary revelation that this beast is a man!

The Rapture of the Saints

This is probably the moment of which Paul speaks, when the dead are raised and the living caught up to heaven (1 Corinthians 15:50 – 54, 1 Thessalonians 4:16 - 17). The cloud could represent the church being taken up with the witnesses. The great earthquake is the same as marked the day of the wrath of the Lamb, when the sixth seal was opened. The earth will reel like a drunkard from the judgements of God, (Isaiah 24:19 – 23, Haggai 2: 6, Hebrews 12:26).

I believe that there will be a very short space of time between the rapture of the church and the return of Christ to establish His kingdom. However I am cautious about fixing a point in prophecy at which the gathering of the church takes place. Jesus said *"Watch therefore for you do not know what hour your Lord is coming"*, and *"the Son of Man is coming at an hour you do not expect."* Matthew 24: 42, 44. We are always to be ready for our Lord's return. It is clear from the Bible that, when He comes, there will be an element of surprise. We are to watch and live in the glorious expectation of His return.

The Third Woe

The coming of the kingdom of Christ is a cause of great celebration to the church, but a woe to the world. Unbelievers know that they will now be judged for their sins. This is the same time as that described when the sixth seal was opened and men hid before the wrath of the Lamb.

In the fifth seal the saints cry, *"When holy and true Master, will you judge and avenge our blood who dwell on the earth?"* The song of the elders in verses 17 and 18 answers this question. The judgement will precede the establishing of Christ's kingdom on earth. When His Kingdom comes the faithful will be rewarded. All believers are now with the Lord and will be able to join in the hymns of praise. He is truly an awesome God. Hallelujah.

Note: The Holy City is trampled for 42 Months. The witnesses prophesy for 1260 days.
The woman (Israel) flees into the wilderness and is protected for 1260 days.
The Beast speaks great things and blasphemies 42 months.

The trampling of the City and the Beast speaking great things, describe the work of Satan and lasts for 42 months. The ministry of the witnesses and the protection of faithful Israel, speak of the work of God and lasts for 1260 days. Both periods add up to three and a half years and refer to the same period. God knows to the day how long He will permit the Antichrist to reign. In all things God remains sovereign, even during this time when Satan appears to have absolute power on earth. Jesus is the ruler over the kings of the earth.

The story of Elijah, who sealed up the heavens for three and a half years, has much to tell us about these last days. Elijah was a forerunner of the two witnesses which God has prepared for the end time.

Christians passing through that time will experience intense persecution. The truth that many will be put to death is not hidden from us. Jesus suffered to pay the penalty for our sin. He invites us to share a little in His suffering that at the very end of this age the whole world will hear the gospel. Our willingness to give up our lives rather than deny our Lord will be a testimony that the world cannot ignore and will also lead to Satan's defeat.

The Last Trumpet

Paul said the church will be caught up (raptured) to be with the Lord at the sounding of the last trumpet (1 Corinthians 15:50-54, 1 Thessalonians 4:16-17).

In the Old Testament there are two times when it is said that God has sounded or will sound a trumpet blast. The first occasion was at Sinai when God made the covenant with Israel (Exodus 19: 16, 19, Hebrews 12: 19). The second time is when God will rescue Israel and gather them to Jerusalem (Isaiah 27:13, Zechariah 9:14).

The Jews referred to these as the first and last trumpets. The first trumpet is remembered at Pentecost when the law was given to Moses. The last is celebrated at the Feast of Trumpets. In the autumn of each year, on the 1st Tishrei, the seventh month of the year, the Jews celebrated Rosh Hashanah, the day for the blowing of Trumpets. It is listed as one of the seven principal feasts of the Israelite year (Leviticus 23:23-25).

The tradition developed that on this day, the Shofar (a ram's horn trumpet) was sounded from the Temple in a set series of blasts. For the preceding 30 days trumpets had been sounded from the Temple as a call to the nation to repent. Rosh Hashanah marked the beginning of a final 10 days when the need to repent becomes more urgent as Yom Kippur, the Day of Atonement, approached. Yom Kippur, the day when those who will not humble themselves before God are cut off from the people, represents to the Jews the Day of Judgement (Leviticus 23:29).

Leviticus does not state why the festival is to be celebrated. It merely says that it is to be a reminder. To the Jews it gained several meanings. Rosh Hashanah literally means 'Head of the Year'. It is the civic New Year. They also believed that on this day *Adam* was created and on Rosh Hashanah the present age will end. It was described as a day of darkness due to it being the only feast to be celebrated at a new moon.

The celebration at the new moon led to a problem in knowing which day the feast should start. Therefore the Rabbis adopted what they called a long day by incorporating the 2nd day of Tishrei into the 1st day in order to be sure that the new moon could be seen and the feast permitted to start. Hence the saying "only the Father in heaven knows the day and hour."

The feast was given a number of other names. One is Ha Melech, the coronation of the Messiah. Trumpets are sounded at the coronation of a king, therefore when God sounds His trumpet it is to proclaim that His Messiah is now king. Another name is Yom Teruah, the day of the awakening blast. The day of the awakening blast referred to the belief that it is on this day that the dead will be raised.

It is possible that Paul is referring to Rosh Hashanah when he speaks of the resurrection and transformation of the dead (1 Corinthians 15: 52, 1 Thessalonians 4: 16). Jesus spoke of the trumpet blast, in terms reminiscent of Isaiah. It will sound when He comes to gather His elect from the four corners of the earth (Isaiah 27: 13, Matthew 24: 31).

ELAH YISRAEL
THE GOD OF ISRAEL

The faithful prophets *Haggai* and *Zechariah* prophesied in the name of the God of Israel to encourage work to continue on the house of God (Ezra 5: 1). It was a word to the persevering remnant not to give up.

REFERENCE	TOPIC	TIMESPAN
Revelation 11: 19 – 12: 6 to **Revelation 12: 13 – 16**	Christ the coming king was born a man to Israel. He watches over the believing remnant of Israel.	The whole history of Israel; but focusing on the very end of the Church Age.

Satan has always hated Israel. They were the people chosen to represent the kingdom of God on earth. This brought them into conflict with Satan's kingdom. Satan targeted Israel persuading them to adopt foreign gods and to be like the surrounding nations. In departing from obedience to God, they transferred their allegiance to the kingdom of this world.

This deception continues to the present day. One thing Satan seeks to prevent, at all cost, is Israel recognizing Jesus as its Messiah. Most in Israel are deceived. Due to not recognizing their Messiah, they are part of the kingdom of this world. Some are secular Jews who have rejected the idea of God. They are Jewish by race, not religion. Then there are the extremely religious, whose hearts are hardened by their traditions and interpretations of the law. There are also, as we have seen, some who seek to serve God but are blind to the truth.

There is another group in Israel whom the Lord cares for. They have come to faith in Jesus Christ as the Messiah. The focus of the prophecies in Revelation now moves to this faithful remnant.

Christ and believing Israel

Revelation 11:19 – 12: 6

The ark of His covenant is seen in heaven in the Temple. According to Hebrews 8: 4 - 5 the earthly tabernacle with its furnishings was a copy of the one in heaven. The Ark of the Covenant symbolizes the covenant with Israel. Lightning, sounds, peals of thunder and earthquake all describe the scene at Sinai when the covenant was given. (Exodus 19:16-19). At Sinai Israel accepted the call to become the people of God. Jeremiah referred to it as a betrothal, (Jeremiah 2: 2).

The woman clothed with the sun

The temple and the ark tell us that the visions have moved on to consider the covenant people of God. That conclusion is confirmed by a second vision; of a woman clothed with the sun and with the moon under her feet and a crown of twelve stars.

The imagery is similar to Joseph's dream (Genesis 37: 9), which refers to Israel and his offspring as the sun, moon and stars. Setting the vision in heaven, tells us that we are dealing with spiritual Israel, not the Israel of this earth.

At the time of Christ's incarnation there was a remnant who we could describe as spiritual Israel. It was made up of those who still trusted the word of God and believed that a Messiah would come. *Mary,* who in faith accepted *Gabriel's* word that she would bear the Messiah, was part of the believing remnant, as was her betrothed *Joseph* who also believed. When Jesus was dedicated in the Temple, *Simeon* and *Anna* declared their faith recognising Jesus as the One who was promised. There may well have been many others in Israel at that time who still believed, but the leaders of the people were not among them. Their attention was focused on the affairs of this world. They were blind to what God was doing.

The interpretation that this refers to believing Israel is also confirmed by the woman bearing a male Child who will rule the nations with a rod of iron. In Psalm 2: 6 – 9, it is Jesus who will rule the nations with a rod of iron. In this vision the Child is caught up to God and His throne. After He died, was buried and rose from the dead, He was taken up to heaven to be seated on the Father's throne.

The hatred of Satan

Satan is seen as a fiery red dragon. Red represents his blood thirsty character. The seven heads, ten horns and diadems describe the mark that he has left on human history. Later we are told that the heads and horns represent kings and empires. It is Satan who has stirred men up to conquer and enslave their fellow man. The stars represent a third of the angelic beings that follow Satan in his rebellion. When he falls to earth, they fall as well.

The dragon, Satan, had an intense hatred for the Child who would one day rule the nations. He knew that this Child would be his undoing. Like a beast watching for its prey he was waiting to devour the Child the moment He was born. Satan used his proxy, **Herod,** to attempt to destroy the baby Jesus (Matthew 2:16). Satan's hatred was poured out on the children of Bethlehem but he failed to achieve his purpose to kill the Son of God. His plans were frustrated when Mary and Joseph escaped with baby Jesus to Egypt.

Satan, cheated of victory, focuses his wrath on Israel who brought the Child into this world. Revelation 12: 6 closes with the woman fleeing into the wilderness for a period of 1260 days.

Verse 6 begins with the conjunction "kai", which means *'and'*. This indicates that the catching up of the male Child, and the woman fleeing, are connected events.

Is this time related? Is it about the Jews being forced out of their land after the ascension of Christ? Forced out due to rejecting their Messiah? Despite that, in exile the Lord preserved them as a nation. Jesus promised that the nation of Israel would not pass away. If so the 1260 days of exile is symbolic, as they were out of the land for over 1800 years.

Believing Israel

Or is it faith related? Another way of connecting the ascension of Christ and the woman fleeing, is to understand that the woman represents the believing remnant of Israel. They are the remnant who recognise Jesus as the Messiah. Because they recognise who Jesus is they will obey His words. When they see the sign of which He warned, they will flee. I think that this is the more likely connection.

Jesus gave a warning that when the 'abomination of desolation' is revealed those in Judea must flee (Matthew 24: 15, 16). The Jews who heed that warning will escape the worst of the reign of the Antichrist.

Our Lord must grieve that so many in Israel do not acknowledge Him as their Messiah. If, down the centuries, they had put their trust in Him, He would have shielded them from much of the trouble they have endured. During this end time it is the same. If only they will listen to His warning, they will be spared. But if they continue in blind disbelief, they will suffer.

Sadly, both the Old and New Testaments testify, that the blindness will continue, until the day on which Jesus physically returns to fight for them (Romans 11: 25). He will come at a time when their power has been shattered and their only remaining hope is to cry out to Him to save them (Daniel 12: 7).

Revelation 12: 13 – 16

We return to the woman. She is persecuted because of bearing the male child and flees to a place of safety in the wilderness. There she will be nourished for time, times and half a time. By describing the period in two ways, once as 1260 days and then as time times and half a time or three and a half years (which is prophetically 1260 days), the passage emphasises that this is to be taken as a literal period and not understood symbolically. It corresponds to the trampling of the holy city, the prophesying of the two witnesses and also to the length of the reign of the beast.

A time to flee

This prophecy is about believing Israel, not natural Israel. When the 'abomination of desolation' appears, believing Israel will obey the warning of Jesus and flee to a place prepared for them. In that place in the wilderness, they will escape the terrible time of anguish, which the rest of their nation will suffer.

Those who flee will be given two wings of an eagle. In Exodus 19:4 the flight from Egypt is described as *"I bore you on eagles' wings, and brought you to Myself"*. The future flight may seem like a desperate escape by any means available, but God will be watching over them. In the wilderness, believing Israel will be looked after by God for the three and a half years of tribulation. Is this place of safety, a country which is free from the reign of the beast, or will they be hidden by Gentile Christians?

Where is the place of Safety?

"But when you see Jerusalem surrounded by armies, then recognise that her desolation is near. Then those who are in Jerusalem must flee to the mountains." Luke 21: 20-21. In this parallel passage in Luke, Jesus is giving a warning of the impending destruction of Jerusalem by the Roman armies. In 66 AD a Roman army under the command of *Cestius Gallus* came up to Jerusalem. After surrounding the city for a week, he withdrew. The leaders of the Jerusalem church recognised this as the sign given by Jesus to warn that it was time to flee. Within their fellowship they had received a prophecy, telling them to flee to Pella on the other side of the Jordan River. The opportunity to escape was short, for soon after the Romans returned to destroy Jerusalem. After the fall of Jerusalem many Jews were executed by the Romans, mainly by crucifixion.

When the abomination of desolation is revealed and the time comes for the faithful remnant to flee, the believers who watch will be guided by the Lord where to go.

Jesus, who is their God, will watch over all who believe His word and obey Him.

ADONAI TSIDKEINU
THE LORD OUR RIGHTEOUSNESS

"THE LORD OUR RIGHTEOUSNESS." is the name Israel will receive during the reign of the Messiah (Jeremiah 23: 6). It is due to the imputed righteousness of Christ that we are able to resist the accusations of the Devil. Therefore it is a name which can be applied to all who overcome whether Jew or Gentile.

REFERENCE	TOPIC	TIMESPAN
Revelation 12: 7–12	How the suffering church contributes to Satan's downfall.	The whole history of mankind but especially the final years of the age.

In the letter to the Colossians, Paul makes a remarkable statement. *"I now rejoice in my sufferings for you, and fill up in my flesh what is lacking in the afflictions of Christ for the sake of His body, which is the church."* Colossians 1:24. Was anything lacking in the sacrifice of Christ? Jesus made full and complete atonement for our sin. In that respect nothing is lacking.

How can we fill up in our flesh what is lacking, if nothing is lacking? Paul had been told that he would suffer many things for the sake of the gospel. (Acts 9: 15 - 16). It was not to add to the atonement that Paul had to suffer. It was to bring to people the hope of the atonement that he suffered. That message, wherever it is preached, brings victory over Satan. It releases captives into the Kingdom of Heaven.

We now move on to a revelation that all who suffer for Christ are achieving victories in the heavenly realms.

Christ and the martyrs
Revelation 12: 7 - 12

A war has broken out in heaven. Michael and the angels are fighting against Satan and his angels. Michael defeats Satan and drives him out of heaven so that there was no longer any place for them there. '*Topos*', the Greek for '*place*' means 'a place marked out'. Satan and his angels are expelled from the territory which they claimed in the heavenly realm. At present these spiritual hosts of wickedness occupy ground in the heavenly places (Ephesians 6: 12). When Michael and the faithful angels bring this to an end, Satan and his host are cast down to the earth to work their evil plans.

It is a time of woe to the earth, because Satan knows that he has only a little time to shore up his crumbling rule. Jesus referred to him as **'the ruler of this world'** (John 14: 30). He has deceived the world into following him. The secularist, the humanist, the evolutionist are already in his camp. They have been deluded into believing that there is no God. The followers of other religions have been deceived into trusting false gods which are no god at all (Isaiah 44: 9 - 20).

There is one group who are not deceived. These are the people who follow Jesus Christ. In these final years, it is Satan's intention to either deceive or intimidate these people into following him. Jesus warned that in the last days, many false christs and false prophets will arise, to deceive if possible even the elect. Satan knows that he has only a short time, in which to eradicate faith in Christ and take control of this world.

The triumph of the saints

Satan is described as, *"the accuser of our brethren, who accused them before our God day and night."* When Satan accused *Job*, he claimed that man would only follow God for material benefit (Job 1: 11, 2: 5) The saints prove this to be a lie. They overcome Satan by being willing to give up everything out of love for their Master. Satan hates those *"who keep the commandments of God and have the testimony of Jesus Christ"* Revelation 12: 17, because their faithfulness has contributed to his defeat. Jesus defined His brethren as *"whoever does the will of My Father in heaven"* Matthew 12: 50.

The testimony of those who overcome Satan is summed up in the following three headings:

And they overcame him by the blood of the Lamb.

Jesus, through His death, destroyed the one who had the power of death (Hebrews 2: 14). Satan had the power of death over us, because we have sinned. Every accusation Satan brings against us is answered by the blood of the Lamb.

Do we allow Satan to attack us and wear us down? He is our adversary, but we are to resist him (1 Peter 5: 8, 9). If we resist him, he will flee (James 4: 7). Satan will have a go because his character is *'the accuser'*. Tell him that everything he says may have been true once, but now all our sin has been cancelled by the blood of the Lamb. There is no other gospel than the atoning sacrifice of Jesus Christ. Those who deny the atonement have no defence against Satan's accusations.

And by the word of their testimony

Satan is defeated when we testify that we have been set free. We are no longer part of his kingdom. We have become part of Christ's kingdom. Jesus said that *"....whoever commits sin is a slave of sin."* John 8: 34. He also said, *"if the Son makes you free, you shall be free indeed."* John 8: 36. Through faith we have been, *"delivered from the power of darkness and conveyed into the kingdom of the Son."* Colossians 1: 13. Jesus came to proclaim release to the captives (Luke 4: 18). Likewise the Lord commissioned Paul to set people free from the power of Satan (Acts 26:18). That is our commission as well. We are either a slave of sin leading to death or of obedience leading to righteousness (Romans 6: 16).

And they did not love their lives even to the death.

Satan is utterly crushed by this. His accusation against us is that we are only in it for what we get out of it. But if people are willing to give up everything for Christ, Satan has no answer.

The final victory

In the 20th Century and continuing into the 21st, millions of Christians have not loved their lives even to death. Some, due to their faith, have lost their livelihood. Others have been falsely accused and thrown into prison. We hear of those who have been enslaved, but refuse to deny their faith. Many have given up their lives. As the end of the age draws closer, the war on the saints will intensify. Every time a person holds fast to their faith in the face of persecution, they are bringing Satan's downfall closer. This is a victory which will be won by the millions of unknown but faithful followers of the Lamb.

Jesus has given us a promise, *"I am with you always, even to the end of the age."* Matthew 28: 20. He will not forsake us in the times of trial. Jesus repeatedly encourages the members of the seven churches to hold fast, persevere and overcome. By holding fast we will have our part in Satan's defeat.

Jesus has won the victory over Satan. He became the perfect sacrifice to atone for our sin. He alone paid that price and is worthy to reclaim the rule over creation. These verses reveal that Jesus will share His glory with all those who stand with Him. All those who make up in their own body the sufferings which prove Satan a liar:

"But thanks be to God, who gives us the victory through our Lord Jesus Christ." 1 Corinthians 15: 57. We acknowledge that it is only through the strength which Christ gives us that we are *"able to stand against the wiles of the devil"* Ephesians 6: 11. Satan's accusations fail because the victory of Jesus over sin is imputed to all who believe, making us righteous in the sight of God.

ELOHEI MA'UZZI
THE GOD OF OUR STRENGTH

Psalm 43 is a prayer to God in a time of trouble. The writer asks for deliverance from an unjust man. In his trouble, God is his strength (Psalm 43: 2). We will need God's strength to stand during the reign of the beast.

REFERENCE	TOPIC	TIMESPAN
Revelation 13: 1–18	Satan's short lived kingdom	The final three-and-a-half years of the present Age.

Will Jesus ever abandon His saints? As this age draws to a close, Satan will be cast out of heaven. Heaven rejoices at Satan's overthrow, but for the earth it heralds a time of woe. Satan is full of wrath at his defeat and knows that he has only a limited time left. This is Satan's last desperate attempt to re-assert his authority on this earth. He is enraged so he turns his hatred against those who contributed to his downfall. They are the saints who keep the commandments of God and have the testimony of Jesus.

For a very brief period at the close of the age, a trinity of evil will be allowed to counterfeit the work of God in order to deceive men. We are warned that the Lord will grant permission to Satan to make war on the saints and overcome them. The saints are called on to be patient and remain faithful. Jesus told us not to fear those who can kill the body (Matthew 10: 28). We are to trust the One who numbers the very hairs of our heads (Luke 12: 7). Satan's final kingdom will be used by God to separate the righteous from the wicked.

Those who place their trust in Jesus can say with Paul, *"for I know whom I have believed and am persuaded that He is able to keep what I have committed to Him until that Day."* 2 Timothy 1: 12. Jesus said that in the world you will have tribulation (John 16: 33). We are to look beyond any present suffering to the glory which will be revealed in us. *"For I consider that the sufferings of this present time are not worthy to be compared with the glory that shall be revealed in us."* Romans 8:21

Christ our strength
Revelation 13: 1 – 18

In a previous vision (Revelation 12: 3) the dragon is described as having seven heads and ten horns. We now see a beast arising out of the sea having these same characteristics. In scripture the organized peoples of the earth are described as the sea or waters (Isaiah 17: 12, Daniel 7: 2, Revelation 17: 15). Since the time of Babel the nations have been divided (Genesis 11: 1- 9). Like the sea there is sometimes calm, sometimes storm. Empires rise and fall like the tides. Nations make war or seek peace. The peace they seek never lasts. This beast will offer the world what it desires but has always eluded it, 'peace'. He will appear so strong that no nation will challenge his rule.

The beast is both an empire and a person. The empire with seven heads and ten horns is the image of Satan. It is intriguing that this imagery seems to be one that Satan accepts. In South East Asia there are many representations of seven headed dragons. Often the dragon heads surround a statue of the Buddha.

The beast which rises out of the sea is further described as, like a leopard with the feet of a bear and the mouth of a lion. This takes us back to Daniel who had a vision of four empires arising from the Great Sea. The first three are likened to a Leopard, a bear and a Lion (Daniel 7: 3 – 7). The beast we now see incorporates these former empires. This beast is a culmination of all the world empires that have gone before it. It is a final world empire at the end of this present age.

The final Empire

In his vision Daniel also saw a fourth beast with ten horns, out of which arises a little horn (Daniel 7: 8). Towards the end of Revelation it is explained that the ten horns represent kingdoms which will give their power to the beast to establish his final empire (Revelation 17: 16 - 17).

The beast is not only an empire, it is also embodied in a person, who will exercise all the authority of Satan on this earth. An empire cannot speak, but a man who heads an empire can. This man speaks great things and blasphemies.

The little horn which arises after the ten horns is described as having *'the eyes of a man and a mouth that spoke boastfully'*. The beast from the sea is identified in the same way, *'speaking great things and blasphemies'*. In his second letter to the Thessalonians Paul writes, *"Don't let anyone deceive you in any way, for that day will not come until the rebellion occurs and the man of lawlessness is revealed, the man doomed to destruction. He will oppose and will exalt himself over everything that is called God or is worshiped, so that he sets himself up in God's temple, proclaiming himself to be God."* 2 Thessalonians 2: 3, 4. The little horn of Daniel, the beast from the sea and the man of sin all represent the same end time dictator who will make war against the kingdom of God. This man totally possessed by Satan is known to Christians as 'the Antichrist'.

The Antichrist is referred to in Isaiah and Jeremiah as *the King of Babylon* (Isaiah 14 and Jeremiah 50) and *the King of Assyria* (Isaiah 10: 5, 12, 30: 31 – 33). The final empire of the Beast will be centred in the Middle East.

There is more to this creature. Satan has healed a fatal wound and raised it from the dead, causing the whole world to wonder. In Revelation 17:11 we learn that the beast empire is a revival of one of the former empires. This revived empire becomes the eighth and final empire of the beast. The world is astonished that the empire, which was thought to be dead, has recovered (Revelation 13: 3). It causes people to worship this empire and ask who can make war with it or, perhaps also to be understood as, who can resist it.

Even more amazing to the world, the leader of this empire will be someone who is brought back from the dead. This is confirmed later in Revelation 17: 8.

In Revelation 13: 5 we read that the beast was given authority for forty two months. The word 'given' should be underlined. 'Given' emphasises that he has no authority unless it is given by God. He speaks great things, boasting of his self-importance but he can only do what God permits. In all that happens, God remains sovereign.

War on the Saints

God's sovereignty is again emphasised in verse 7 where we read, *"It was granted to him"*. Proclaiming himself as God, the beast is for a time allowed to make war on the followers of Christ. Daniel 7: 21 warns that the faithful will be overcome by the little horn/beast.

Revelation opens with letters to seven churches. Each letter has an exhortation *"to him who overcomes"*, followed by a promise. One purpose of Revelation is to encourage us to overcome. There is a clear warning that in this final time many will be martyred or imprisoned. We are called on to persevere and promised that if we do we will be blessed. As Christians we must be prepared to suffer for our Lord, while at the same time living in the expectant blessed hope of Christ's return. We will overcome if we do not rely on our own strength but look to Christ who strengthens us (Philippians 4: 13).

"if anyone has ears to hear let him hear" is a reference to the prophecy most frequently quoted in the Bible. It is found in Isaiah 6: 9, 10. The people of Israel were condemned for having ears but not listening. Therefore they lacked understanding and didn't return to the Lord. We must not to be like them. We need to listen to prophecy so that we are prepared and not deceived.

The Trinity of Evil

Revelation commenced with John in prayer for the Christians he loved. If they refused to bow down to Caesar, they faced persecution and death. At the very end of this age, Christians will face the same pressure. It is decreed that all that will not worship the image of the beast be killed. To force all dissent into the open, those who do not submit to the ruler, will suffer economic isolation.

In the new Heaven and new Earth, Jesus will rule through love. There will be no force, because all who are part of His kingdom love Him, and will gladly do His will. In contrast, Satan can only rule through fear. Being the father of lies and deceit he can trust no one (John 8: 44). The world will now experience what has been true all along. If God is rejected, the only alternative is an absolute totalitarian state where people are forced to do the will of the leader. Every one, no matter what their status, will come under the control of the Antichrist.

"He performs great signs". People look for supernatural signs to confirm the truth (Matthew 12: 39, 1 Corinthians 1: 22). Satan will satisfy their craving and use this weakness to deceive them.

We have a trinity of evil at work, which in their different functions imitate the true trinity of Father, Son and Holy Spirit. The dragon, Satan, imitates the Father. Satan initiated the rebellion against God and continues to lead it. The *beast from the Sea* or *Antichrist* imitates the Son, being the visible expression of his father the Devil. We are now introduced to another member of the trinity, a second beast who is later called *the false prophet.* The Holy Spirit convicts of sin, reveals truth and brings people to the true worship of God and His Son Jesus Christ. The false prophet counters this work by confirming sin, speaking lies and leading people to worship the beast. He is able to work great miracles in order to deceive the world into worshipping the beast.

The Holy Spirit is known by His work. He is not visible to us (John 3:8). In the same way the false prophet will be recognizable by his work. He is a demonic spiritual power intimately connected with Satan and carrying out his work on earth.

God created man in His own image and breathed into him the breath of life so that he became a living being (Genesis 2: 7). Satan deceived man to fall from his position of favour with God. Christians are regenerated through the work of the Holy Spirit and restored to the image of God (Colossians 3: 10). When they are born again the breath of God the Holy Spirit enters them to give them new life. God places a seal on all his servants, (2 Corinthians 1: 22, Ephesians 4: 30). They are known to Him and loved by Him.

The false prophet imitates the work of the Holy Spirit. He corrupts men's hearts and deceives them into becoming the image of Satan. He breathes his demonic power into them condemning them to death. Full of hatred these men speak the words of Satan, killing all those who will not submit to their master the devil.

The above interpretation sees a fulfilment not in a literal image, but the image of Satan created in people's hearts. This view is taken, because it fits with the identifying of the roles of the trinity of evil, as mirroring the work of the Holy Trinity. In every respect Satan seeks to counterfeit the work of God. He wishes to be God but knows no other on which to model himself.

This may be only part of the truth. It is possible that a literal image will be constructed. Satan, through the work of the false prophet, may engage in his own act of creation appearing to turn an inanimate statue into a living being. The Bible says that he was **granted** this power, once again emphasizing that God is sovereign.

On the plain of Dura, *King Nebuchadnezzar* constructed a golden image (Daniel 3:1). He commanded that all the people should bow down in worship to the image. If they would not worship the image they were to be thrown into the furnace. Daniel 3 tells the story of **Shadrach, Meshach** and **Abednego** who refuse to worship anyone but their God. They are thrown into the furnace, from which, to the amazement of Nebuchadnezzar, their God delivered them. This story is a great encouragement to those who know that by refusing to worship the beast they will face death. There is certainty, that even if we die, God will deliver us.

The Mark

The Christian bears the seal of God which declares that we are Christ's. The mark of the beast is Satan's counterfeit of the seal of God. Acceptance of his name, mark or number is an acknowledgement of Satan's ownership. In the next chapter we will learn that those who accept the mark will share Satan's fate.

Most people focus on the number of the beast. However if the line of argument has been followed, first that the beast comes from the Abyss, second that he had once lived on this earth and been killed, the most startling statement in Revelation 13: 18 is the confirmation that this beast is a man.

Antichrist, Resurrected?

The first mention of '*the beast*' is in Revelation 11:7. It is evidently the same creature as mentioned in Revelation 13:1 and 17:8, and is doubtless that *"little horn"* spoken of by Daniel *"which made war against the saints and prevailed against them"* (Daniel 7: 8 – 21). It is written he ascends out of the bottomless pit (Revelation 11: 7, 17: 8). This beast is the Antichrist who now manifests himself in all of his diabolical power as the man of sin (2 Thessalonians 2: 3).

Abaddon is the only one who is mentioned by name as being released from the bottomless pit (Revelation 9: 11). So is the beast Abaddon, who has been imprisoned in the abyss until the time is right to release him?

Later in Revelation the beast is again described. Once again reference is made to his coming from the bottomless pit. This time we are told that he, *"The beast that you saw was and is not and will ascend out of the bottomless pit and go to perdition,.....the beast that was and is not and yet is.",* Revelation 17:8, indicating that the beast had been on this earth before the time that Revelation was written and will return in the future.

Many in the early church believed that it would be the *Emperor Nero* who would return from the bottomless pit. He had been killed with a sword stroke. I believe that if we are looking for a man who has been imprisoned in the pit for two thousand years, there is another more likely candidate. (See Appendix 1).

It is not proposed that Satan can give life. But can Satan bring back from the pit a life that previously existed? The answer to that question is, only if Jesus permits. (1 Samuel 28:7-25 is interesting in this respect). And Jesus will permit it only if it serves His purposes.

Second Thessalonians confirms this: *"And you know what restrains him now, so that in his time he may be revealed. For the mystery of lawlessness is already at work; only He who now restrains will do so until He is taken out of the way."* 2 Thessalonians 2: 6 – 7. If translated literally *'until He is taken out of the way'* becomes *'until out of the midst he comes'*. The verse is not speaking of someone being removed but someone being revealed. A literal rendering of this verse solves the question of who is restraining the mystery of lawlessness. Jesus has the power to decide who is consigned to the bottomless pit, also called the abyss (Luke 8: 31). He also has the keys to death and all the unseen world (Revelation 1: 18) from which the man of lawlessness is to be released. Jesus will restrain until the time comes for Him to hand over the key to Satan to open the bottomless pit. Therefore verses 6 and 7 say the same thing and have a similar balance. The verses are set out below to illustrate the meaning:

6a And now you know the thing holding back, (the power of Jesus)
6b for him to be revealed in his time.　　　　　　(the Antichrist)
For the mystery of lawlessness is already working;
7a Only He holding back now,　　　　　　　　(Jesus)
7b until it comes out of the midst.　　　　　(the Antichrist)

Paul is reassuring the Christians at Thessalonica by emphasizing that the man of lawlessness can only be revealed at the time when Jesus permits. He is not saying that Christians will escape that time. Instead he repeats twice, to stress that when the Antichrist appears, it will be in accordance with the will of Jesus. The revealing of the Antichrist heralds a time of great trouble but it is also the assurance of the soon return of Christ.

Christ our Strength

"Not that I speak in regard to need, for I have learned in whatever state I am in to be content: I know how to be abased and I know how to abound. Everywhere and in all things I have learned both to be full and to be hungry, both to abound and to suffer need. I can do all things through Christ who strengthens me." Philippians 4: 11 – 13.

Refusing the mark of the beast, which will lead to being an outcast from society, is not a welcome prospect. The apostle Paul learned that the answer to such situations, is to look to Jesus Christ for our strength. He will not forsake us.

REVELATIONS OF JESUS CHRIST

EL ELYON
THE MOST HIGH GOD

"Yet they tested and provoked the Most High God, and did not keep His testimonies." Psalm 78: 56. Due to disobedience Israel was punished. The Psalm goes on to say that God was furious (Psalm 78: 59). The Most High God repeatedly warned Israel of the consequence of their rebellion. The word of this same Most High God now warns the world that there will be a time of retribution for its rebellion.

REFERENCE	TOPIC	TIMESPAN
Revelation 14: 6–20	Final warning to this world followed by two harvests, one of wheat and the other of weeds.	The close of the Church Age.

Jesus opened His ministry with a quotation from Isaiah. He started with the words *"The Spirit of the Lord is upon me"* and ended with, *"to proclaim the favourable year of the Lord"*. Luke 4: 18 – 19. The prophecy in Isaiah 61: 2 continues with the words *"And the day of vengeance of our God"*. When will this day of vengeance come?

For the last 2000 years we have lived in a time of God's favour. It has been a time when the gospel has been taken to all nations. A time when the way of salvation has been offered to all people. But the favourable day of the Lord will not last for ever. There will come a day when our God pours out His vengeance on a rebellious sinful world. Jesus is now revealed as the One who reaps the harvest of the earth.

Christ the reaper
Revelation 14: 6 - 20

This section opens with three warnings of coming vengeance. The first warning is the gospel preached to all who dwell on the earth. The second warning is the fall of Babylon. The final warning is the reign of the beast, which we looked at in the previous chapter.

The gospel preached to all people

Jesus said, *"This gospel of the kingdom will be preached in all the world as a witness to all nations and then the end will come."* Matthew 24: 14. Before judgment can come the followers of Christ must complete the commission to *"Go into all the world and preach the gospel to every creature."* Mark 16: 15.

John sees an angel flying in heaven with the everlasting gospel to be preached to all who dwell on the earth. The gospel having been preached, God is looking for a response. The angel calls on people everywhere to, *"Fear God and give the glory to Him"* and to *"worship Him who made the heaven and earth, the sea and springs of water."* The world needs to hear that God is both Creator and Judge.

It is noteworthy that the challenge that God lays before mankind is to recognise Him as Creator. We live in an age when men have rejected the idea of a Creator. According to "scientific" mythology, existence is due to a random process guided by what is called 'natural selection'. Current reasoning says that if we are the product of natural processes there is no God. Therefore there is neither any need to fear God nor give Him glory. As there is no judge, there is no one to hold anyone to account. Rejection of the Creator has led to the denial of the distinctive nature of man created as male and female. Gender confusion is but one sign that we are nearing the end of this age.

The theory of evolution has become the greatest stumbling block to belief in God. Mass rejection of God as Creator is a sign of impending wrath.

We are to give God the glory for He is both Creator and Judge. In preparing the way for Jesus Christ, *John the Baptist* preached repentance. The primary message of the faithful, when preparing for Christ's return, should also be repent. Repentance that we have not given God the honour and glory due to Him as our Creator. The apostate church cannot preach this eternal gospel. It has sided with the world in denying God as Creator and portrays Him as One who will not judge.

Scripture is clear. The gospel will be preached to all people and then rejected. The rulers of this world will be entrenched in their opposition to Christ. Instead of turning to Jesus for wisdom they will look to a false god for guidance. When Jesus returns He will not be met with rejoicing but by opposition to His reign. In response God will pour out His wrath. With the rejection of the gospel by the nations, the age of God's favour draws to a close.

The fall of Babylon
The second warning of coming judgement is the fall of Babylon. The identity of Babylon is dealt with in more detail in Revelation chapters 17 and 18. Here it is sufficient to say that *Babylon* is what men call *civilisation*. God calls it *the kingdom of this world*.

It is most clearly manifested today in the western world. The West has achieved wealth and power beyond the dreams of former ages. At the close of this age the kingdom of this world will experience sudden collapse. According to the Bible, in one hour she will be made desolate and her great riches will come to nothing.

The total collapse of its economic strength, destroying its self-reliance, is a warning from God of the emptiness of all that man aspires to. The angel proclaims that Babylon's fall is God's judgment. It is also a sign that the time is drawing close when God will pour out His wrath.

The final warning
The fall of Babylon will lead into the time of terrible destruction through war that is described in Revelation chapter 9. In desperation men will cry out for a deliverer. But instead of turning to God they will accept Satan's man.

The kingdom of the beast is the final warning to humanity that the time of God's favour is coming to an end. His vengeance is soon to be poured out.

If people choose the rule of Satan instead of God, there is no longer any mercy. By receiving his mark, they have sided with the enemy of God and will accordingly be treated as His enemies. Those who worship the beast and his image will be tormented and have no rest day or night. This judgment takes place when Jesus returns at the end of the time of tribulation. It is the same judgment as that described in Matthew 25: 31 - 46. The 'goats', who I believe to be the same as those who receive the mark of the beast, are thrown into the everlasting fire prepared for the devil and his angels.

The Endurance of the Saints

During these times, the saints are called on to be patient and to persevere (Luke 21: 19). We are called to walk the same path as He walked. So that by our faithful witness some will be saved from the judgment to come. Those who keep the commandments of God and faith in Jesus during this time will be blessed. The striving of this present age will give way to rest.

"Blessed are the dead who die in the Lord from now on." There will be a time of suffering in which many of the faithful will die. If we are called to give up our lives, there is a promise from God, that He will greatly reward all that hold true in this time of trial. Faithfulness during a brief time of suffering will reap eternal rewards (Romans 8: 17, 2 Corinthians 4: 17, 1 Peter 4: 13).

How will we endure? *"...let us run with endurance the race that is set before us, looking unto Jesus"*. Hebrews 12: 1. We will complete the race by keeping our eyes fixed on Jesus. Contrary to our natural inclinations, the Bible presents suffering for Christ as a privilege.

From the beginning we have known that the followers of Jesus will be hated by the world. Jesus said that *"you will be hated by all for My name's sake."* Luke 21: 17. He calls on us to be patient and adds that not even a hair of our head will be lost (Luke 21: 18, 19).

In Romans 8: 16 – 18 we read that the sufferings in this life bear no comparison to the glory of the next, while Philippians 1: 29 says that suffering is something granted by God.

The Wheat Harvest

Having heard the third angel make the proclamation of judgement, John, in the vision, now witnesses it being carried out.

In answering the High Priest, at His trial, Jesus said: *"you will see the Son of Man ...... coming with the clouds."* Mark 14: 62. Jesus was identifying Himself with the prophecy in Daniel 7: 13 – 14. In that prophecy *"One like the Son of Man, coming with the clouds of heaven"* receives an everlasting kingdom and dominion over all peoples. He was saying that; *I am the One who will one day reign over all peoples.* No wonder the High Priest was furious.

In Revelation 14 we learn that the first harvest will be by the Lord Himself. The *One like the Son of Man,* who will rule over the nations, will first reap the harvest of the faithful. He is also called *the good shepherd* who knows His own sheep (John 10: 14). No one, who should be in his safe keeping, will be forgotten.

Jesus told a parable about a harvest (Matthew 13: 24 – 30). His explanation of its meaning is found in Matthew 13: 37 – 43. In the parable the field is the world and therefore the harvest will be worldwide. It will take place at the end of this age. It is a separation between the sons of the Kingdom and the sons of the wicked one. The righteous will shine like the sun in the kingdom of their Father. The fruit of this harvest is seen in Revelation 15: 1 – 4.

The Harvest of the Tares

The Lord gathers His own but, as in Matthew 13, He leaves it to the angels to gather the wicked. Having gathered His sheep to a place of safety, the command is given to reap the other harvest which is the judgment of the wicked. They are the tares in the parable of the wheat and the tares. Satan sows them, and as his sons they conform to his image.

This harvest of tares is preceded by the outpouring of the bowls of wrath, which is described in the next chapter of Revelation. In this chapter we read how the wrath culminates with the gathering of grapes, previously described as *tares,* to be thrown into the winepress of God's fury. The final crushing of the rebellion will take place at the battle of Armageddon which follows the reign of the beast. In that battle the armies of this world will be trampled (Isaiah 63: 1 – 6, Joel 3: 12 – 16). Following Armageddon the wicked are gathered, bound, judged and burnt.

ELOHIM

GOD THE STRONG ONE

That God has allowed mankind to go his own way for so long is not due to weakness. His name, used 2570 times in the *Tanakh* (Old Testament), means the strong one. It is plural, for it represents Father, Son and Holy Spirit. The world will discover His strength when it experiences the full force of His anger.

REFERENCE	TOPIC	TIMESPAN
Revelation 15: 5 to Revelation 16: 21	The wrath of God is a last call to repentance.	The close of the Church Age.

Is God a benign 'Father Christmas' figure sitting on the clouds up in heaven? If you think so please read on. This is a revelation of Jesus Christ in which He does not appear. It is His absence which is to be noted. His Father's wrath is now poured out on a sinful world. He is angry that the people have rejected the sacrifice of His beloved Son.

The Father's Wrath

Revelation 15: 5 – 16: 21

The Tabernacle in the wilderness contained the Ark of the Covenant. Inside the ark were the tablets with the commandments of God on them (1 Kings 8:9). The angels coming from the tabernacle signify that the judgements are on an evil world, ruined by man's disobedience to the commandments of God. The people of this world have not given the glory to God and worshipped the One, *"who made heaven and earth, the sea and the springs of water."*

We have now reached the limit of the patience and mercy of God. Once the day of judgement has come, smoke prevents anyone entering the Temple to intercede on behalf of the suffering.

What follows, is similar to the trumpet judgements, only more intense. These judgements are no longer the work of evil angels. *They are the direct wrath of God poured out by faithful angels on a wicked earth.* It is a dreadful picture of suffering in which bodies are covered with painful sores, the seas die, and water becomes undrinkable. This is divine retribution for millennia of rebellion and persecution of the faithful.

"You are righteous, O Lord". The angels recognize that in this judgment God is acting justly. The saints are not to seek revenge for the injustice that has been suffered in this life. It is God who will judge (Romans 12: 19 – 20, Hebrews 10: 30 – 31). We are to warn people that when God repays evil, His judgment is terrible.

Three times over in this passage (verses 9, 11, 21) the response of men to the plagues sent by God is not repentance but to blaspheme His name. They blame God not themselves for all that is happening to them.

The earth will reel under this outpouring of wrath (Isaiah 24: 19 – 23, Haggai 2: 6, Hebrews 12: 26). It will be terrifying to experience the planet swaying from side to side.

Armageddon

It is not ignorance that separates man from God but wickedness. The saints have gone and the world is suffering the judgment of a righteous God. Instead of repenting, spurred on by the evil trinity, mankind makes a final futile effort to dislodge God from this world and claim it as their own.

God will gather the nations of the world to the valley of Jehoshaphat (Joel 3: 2, 12). There He will enter into judgment against them. God allows demonic powers to stir the nations to war but He is the One who decrees how this conflict will end. 'Jehoshaphat' means *YHWH judges*.

We have a double emphasis on what comes out of the mouth. The evil spirits come out of the mouth of the dragon. They are described as frogs. Frogs catch their prey with their tongues. It is by speaking lies and falsehood that the spirits stir up the nations to war.

A warning is inserted in verse 15 to beware, lest by failing to be vigilant, believers come under the outpouring of God's wrath. All the references in the New Testament to Jesus coming as a thief, warn of the danger of losing what is rightfully ours. (Matthew 24:36 – 25:30. Luke 12: 39 – 40, 1 Thessalonians 5:2, Revelation 3:3).

At this point in time the faithful should be with our Lord enjoying His presence and preparing for His return. We should not be suffering the terrible judgement of God. 'Going naked' speaks of an empty worldly form of faith. It pays lip service to the worship of God but does not come from the heart. A time will come when the emptiness is exposed for all to see. Through true faith in Christ we are clothed in His righteousness and will never be ashamed.

The day of the Lord

The bowls of wrath and the gathering of the world to Armageddon combine to become what the Old Testament frequently refers to as *'the Day of the Lord'* (Isaiah 13: 6 – 13, 24: 1 – 23, 63: 1 – 6, Joel 2: 3 – 3: 3, 3: 9 – 21, Amos 5: 18 – 20, Zephaniah 1: 14 – 18, Zechariah 14: 1 – 8). The Prophets of Israel often spoke of a time when the Lord would come in judgment. It would be a terrible day when God acts in judgment on a rebellious world.

"It is done".

When the seventh bowl is poured out a loud voice comes from the throne declaring *"it is done"*. This day ends the judgement of God on this evil world.

The duration of the wrath

How long will the outpouring of wrath last? It is possible that the wrath of God will last for no longer than the 10 days, which separate Rosh Hashanah (the Feast of Trumpets) from Yom Kippur (the Day of Atonement).

In the Hebrew calendar there are three autumn feasts, Rosh Hashanah on the first day of the seventh month, Yom Kippur on the tenth day and Sukkot (Tabernacles) which begins on the fifteenth day (Leviticus 23: 23 – 44).

Rosh Hashanah is, according to Jewish tradition, *the day of the last Trumpet.* It is looked on by the Jews as the feast when the Messiah will come and the dead are raised. Yom Kippur is a *day of judgement*, when according to the Law those who are not repentant are cut off from the people of God. Between the two feasts are 10 days, known as Yamim Noraim (the days of awe), when the call to repent becomes urgent.

The outpouring of wrath is a retribution on sin. It is also a final plea from God to repent before it is too late. Could the world stand more than a few days of His wrath?

"And Great Babylon was remembered before God"

The word translated 'remembered', referring to Babylon the Great, is used one other time in the New Testament. *"Cornelius, your prayer has been heard and your alms have been remembered before God"* Acts 10: 31. In that context it refers to a reward for past actions.

Babylon's past actions are remembered by God as being thoroughly evil. At this time, Babylon has already fallen, but retribution for her sins was not complete. The outpouring of wrath, which will affect her as well as the beast kingdom, is the just reward for all the evil of Babylon the Great (the kingdom of this world), over thousands of years.

ELOHEI MISHPAT
THE GOD OF JUSTICE

"For the Lord is a God of justice; blessed are those who wait for Him". Isaiah 30: 18. A day is coming when God will judge the kingdom of this world for all her sins. Then the kingdom of Heaven will rejoice and dwell in peace.

REFERENCE	TOPIC	TIMESPAN
Revelation 17 and Revelation 18	A look at the fate of the kingdom of this world, the great enemy of God and persecutor of the saints throughout the ages.	Babylon falls just before the Kingdom of the Beast is established.

When the fifth seal is opened the Martyrs cry out, *"How long, O Lord, holy and true, until You judge and avenge our blood on those who dwell on the earth?"* They had been persecuted, mistreated and killed by the kingdom of this world. They cry out to the God of justice, when will the evil be avenged? It is not for us to avenge ourselves. Only the Lord can judge with absolute knowledge. With our imperfect understanding it is all too easy for us to condemn the innocent. *"Beloved, do not avenge yourselves, but rather give place to wrath; for it is written, "Vengeance is Mine, I will repay," says the Lord."* Romans 12: 19. The quote comes from Deuteronomy 32: 35, which assures us that a day of calamity will come on the wicked. They will receive recompense from God for their evil deeds. That day of retribution is now revealed. It is a day when Christ who is just and righteous punishes the kingdom of this world for *"the blood of prophets and saints and all who were slain on the earth."* Revelation 18: 24.

Revelation ends with a vision of the New Jerusalem, the bride of Christ. But first we are told of the fate of her opposite, Babylon the Great, the harlot bride of Satan. The New Jerusalem is made up of all those who have trusted Christ as their Redeemer. Babylon the Great comprises all that hate God and reject His ways. The New Jerusalem is the Kingdom of God. Those who faithfully represented the Kingdom of God in this present age belong to her. Babylon the Great is the kingdom of this world. She stands in opposition to the truth.

John says in his first letter, *"the whole world lies under the sway of the wicked one"* 1 John 5:19. Strong words, but in this vision the truth of that statement unfolds in stark reality. Christians need to see the world as God sees it, and listen to the words He spoke through John. *"Do not love the world or the things in the world. If anyone loves the world, the love of the Father is not in him. For all that is in the world, the lust of the flesh, the lust of the eyes and the pride of life is not of the Father but is of the world. And the world is passing away, and the lust of it; but he who does the will of God abides forever."* 1 John 2: 15 – 17.

The Babylon story covers the same period of world history as the vision of the Seals, from Cain's rebellion to the return of Christ. For the whole of that period there is constant warfare between the kingdom of God and the kingdom of this world.

In scripture, Babylon represents an oppressive world empire that triumphed over the people of God (2 Chronicles 36: 17 – 21). Rooted in an historical rebellion, it became a symbol for any organised structure, which attempts to replace God's kingdom with a human or demonic substitute (Isaiah 47, Jeremiah 50:29-32).

This prophecy of her fall is in retrospect. The beast and the ten kingdoms cause the downfall of Babylon the Great (Revelation 17: 16). Her removal is necessary to clear the way for their rise to power. In the order of events, the downfall of Babylon the Great takes place before the coming of the beast. However it is necessary to take the kingdom of the beast and the wrath of God first, in order to explain the context of the fall of Babylon. Placing the destruction of Babylon at this point in the prophecy, underlines the seriousness with which God regards Babylon's sin. The Kingdom of the Beast was evil and had to be destroyed, but it is the sins of Babylon, which are the cause of God bringing this present age to an end.

Christ the Just

Revelation 17: 1 - 18

To find out what, MYSTERY BABYLON THE GREAT, MOTHER OF HARLOTS AND OF THE ABOMINATIONS OF THE EARTH." represents, we will look at her character as described in Revelation.

First we learn that God hates her, (Revelation 16: 19). Then in chapter 17 verses 1 to 6 we are told the following about her:

1). She is described as a great harlot. (Jerusalem was called a harlot when she abandon the true God for the worship of false gods, Isaiah 1: 21).

2). By her fornication she has led the rulers and peoples of the earth astray teaching them to worship other gods.

3). Having corrupted many others she is called the Mother of Harlots.

4). She revels in all that God finds to be an abomination.

5). She sits on many waters. In verse 15 this is interpreted as peoples, multitudes, nations and tongues.

She led the rulers and peoples of the earth astray to worship other gods. She is seated on the beast. She is not the same as the beast but relies on the beast for her considerable wealth and security. She persecutes those who are faithful to Jesus and is the source of all the corruption in the earth. Later we learn how she glorifies herself and is filled with pride.

'*Sitting on many waters*' is a reference to her influence spreading over the entire earth. Through deception and worship of the false god Satan she has amassed great wealth and luxury. This is expanded on later in the prophecy where we learn that despite her outward show of wealth she is the home of demons and every foul spirit.

A literal city?

Several times she is called 'that great city'. Is this a reference to a literal city? We are also told that she sits on seven mountains. Rome, London, New York and Mecca are all said to be built on seven hills. But can any literal city be the source of all the corruption in the earth?

Her wealth and trade make her more than a purely religious system. Her harlotry makes her more than just the world economy. She has existed longer than any end time world government, for in her is found the blood of all slain on the earth. She is older and more extensive than Europe. The woman is not the same as the individual empires. The beast on which she rides has seven heads representing the empires of this world. Her adulterous relationship is with them all spanning the whole of history.

There is no single city which fits her character. In the light of the huge rejoicing in heaven at her fall and the global significance of her trade, Babylon represents something much bigger than a single city, country, empire or even a religious system. That is why I believe that she represents *the kingdom of this world*.

The birth of civilisation

A clue which confirms her identity is found in Revelation 18: 24 ***"And in her was found the blood of prophets and saints and all who were slain on the earth"***. This takes us back to the time of the first murder. In Genesis we read that *Cain* killed his brother *Abel*. Abel's offering of the first born from his flock was accepted but Cain's was rejected (Genesis 4: 5). Cain knew what was acceptable to God but did not bring it. He was angry with God because the ground had been cursed and now produced thorns and thistles. To bring an acceptable offering to God was hard toil.

Out of jealousy he kills his brother. As a punishment Cain is condemned to be a fugitive, with a warning that from now on tilling the ground will be even harder work. Cain wanted the blessings of God without obedience. Now his punishment is greater than he can bear. Driven from the presence of God he fears that he will be killed. God promises that he will be protected. Cain goes out from the presence of the Lord and settles in the land of Nod.

There he builds a city. People have always regarded cities as places of safety. A place where they can defend themselves from their enemies. Cain is trusting in himself for protection rather than God.

After five generations *Lamech* is born into this city. He is first to break with God's divinely appointed order of one man one wife. It is interesting that the offspring of this rebellious relationship are very creative (Genesis 4: 20 – 22). *Jabal* develops agriculture. *Jubal* is into the arts, developing music. *Tubal-Cain* is a metal worker. With the arts, technology and agriculture 'civilisation' is born to this ungodly line.

In Revelation 18: 22 music and technology, which we used to identify Babylon as representing civilisation, are brought to an end when Babylon falls, confirming the link back to Lamech.

When mankind has developed new technologies, what is the first use he usually puts it to? Lamech, boasts that he has killed a younger [i.e. stronger] man. His son's metal work has enabled the production of weapons. With weapons Lamech can boast, we no longer need God. Soon the world was filled with violence (Genesis 6: 13).

What we call civilisation came out of Cain's rebellion. 'Civilisation' becomes the focus of rebellion against God.

A new world, the same rebellion

Because of the violence filling the earth, God brings the flood and creates a fresh start. However four generations on from *Noah, Nimrod* was born. He is described as a mighty hunter against the Lord. He founded a kingdom and gave protection to people from the animal kingdom which was going wild (Gen 10: 8 – 12). His first city was called Babel. Nimrod's Babel soon became the source of all false religion. Babel later named Babylon fits the description of the MOTHER OF HARLOTS.

The command of God to Noah and his sons was to go out and fill the earth (Genesis 9: 1). Instead, God finds men gathering together into cities. The same rebellion was starting up again. The city, and particularly the city called Babel becomes a symbol of man's rebellion against God (Genesis 11: 1 – 9).

Two kingdoms are now in conflict, *the kingdom of this world* and the *kingdom of God*. Jerusalem was called by God to represent His kingdom. When she sinned God used Babylon to punish her disobedience. Babylon will always triumph when the citizens of God's kingdom are disobedient. For Isaiah and Jeremiah, Babylon becomes the personification of wickedness.

The beast

The beast on which the Harlot rides is the manifestation of Satan the god of this world. His power comes through kingdoms and empires. Satan's blasphemy is to exalt himself above God (Isaiah 14: 12 – 14). The woman is captivated by the wealth Satan offers. She does not care what level of abomination and fornication she sinks to, provided there is wealth as represented by purple, scarlet, gold and precious stones. In this she is the mother of all empires and civilizations to follow. Their quest for wealth and power at the expense of justice and humanity is an abomination to God. Heads represent empires and horns represent nations.

Babylon in all its forms hates those who keep faith with the living God. Their witness to the truth condemns her. Throughout history she has opposed the faithful and shed their blood.

What is Babylon today?

Revelation takes the Old Testament imagery of Babylon as the personification of wickedness and rebellion and applies it to the culmination of man's pride at the end of the age.

At the end of Revelation there is a vision of the New Jerusalem, the bride of Christ. Her opposite number is Babylon the Great, the harlot bride of Satan. All who have trusted Christ as their Redeemer belong to the New Jerusalem. Those that hate God and reject His ways are citizens of Babylon.

For men, cities display their strength. In the city the arts thrive, there is music, architecture and theatre and philosophy. The city with its resources gives opportunity to develop technology. City society is ordered and regulated by manmade laws. Cities have armies for defence and war.

Babylon is man's attempt the live independently from God. She is the kingdom of this world, what we would call civilisation. She has a facade of greatness, but underneath she is proud and corrupt, seeking wealth by any means.

The Babylon story covers world history, from Cain to the return of Christ. For the whole of that period there has been constant warfare between the kingdom of God and the kingdom of this world. Babylon becomes a symbol for any organised structure that attempts to replace God's kingdom with a human or demonic substitute.

We have a choice, to which kingdom do we want to belong? (1 John 2: 15 – 17).

At the end of her days Babylon has become preoccupied with money. She has enticed the leaders and the peoples of the world to follow after her in the pursuit of luxury.

Babylon is a trading power filled with pride. She says she sits as a queen. All the merchants and those who have grown rich through trade with her will mourn when she falls.

God has allowed men to adopt symbols in order to make things easier for us. The European Union adopted the symbol of *Europa* as a political statement. The old Judeo/Christian culture is discarded in favour of pagan Greek culture. In sculpture and pictures she is portrayed as a woman riding a beast.

European/Greek culture dominates the modern world. In Bible terms it sits on many waters. In these closing years of the present age, it is the western world which best fits the description of Babylon the Great.

The leaders of the world and the nations aspire to share in Babylon's wealth. For man she is the pinnacle of civilisation. But in the sight of God, she is evil, corrupt and soon to fall. She is anti-God seeking to reverse the judgment of Babel.

At the opening of chapter 17 John is invited to witness the judgment of the harlot. The description of the beast is included in the chapter so that we understand its important role in the destruction of the harlot. Babylon's fall comes before and makes way for the reign of the beast.

If global trade collapsed, so would civilisation as we know it. The world would quickly descend into lawlessness. The collapse of civilisation will cause men to look to the Beast for salvation. But note it is all in accordance with the will of God.

Nebuchadnezzar had to learn, *"...that the Most High rules in the kingdom of men and gives it to whomever He will."* Daniel 4: 17. Christ is both King of Kings and the Judge of all kingdoms.

Hate for the Harlot

There is a surprise twist to the story. While Jesus cherishes His bride and looks forward to spending eternity with her, Satan comes to hate his harlot wife and destroys her. She is destroyed in order to make way for the beast kingdom, which then strips her of her wealth.

We must emphasise that the beast empire and the harlot are not the same. In the three final warnings, Babylon falls to make way for the kingdom of the beast. This is confirmed in Revelation 17: 16 – 17 where the ten nations which arise at the end time to give their power to the beast will destroy the harlot. God is sovereign. He puts it in their hearts to do this.

In the description of the beast, the seven kings refers to the seven empires which have overshadowed the history of Israel. The first was Egypt, followed by Assyria, Babylon, Persia and Greece. These five had fallen at the time John received this revelation. Rome is referred to as 'one is'. The empire which succeeded Rome in ruling the Holy Land was Islam. That empire finally came to an end in 1924 with the removal of the Caliph.

At the end of the age the seventh of the empires which was Islam will be revived to become the eighth empire. Islam hates all other religions and the corrupt nations of the Western world. When Islam gains power it will seek to destroy those nations and religions.

This final empire is described as ten horns that are given power for only one hour. They are granted authority for one purpose only; to establish the kingdom of the beast. The kingdom of the beast, as a rebirth of a former empire, will amaze the world. The beast is also a person who, *"will ascend out of the bottomless pit and go to perdition."* He *"was and is not"*. As noted in a previous chapter, if we take this literally, at the time Revelation was written, the man who is to become the beast had been alive but was currently dead. He will come back to life.

The warfare against the kingdom of God will reach its greatest intensity during this period, but the victory of Jesus is assured.

Revelation 18:1 - 24

Whatever else Babylon the Great may have been, at the end of her days she has become preoccupied with money. She has enticed the leaders and the peoples of the world to follow after her in the pursuit of luxury. Money in itself does not lead to happiness. It is an empty goal leading to many types of evil. *"But those who desire to get rich fall into temptation and a snare and into many foolish and harmful lusts which drown men in destruction and perdition. For the love of money is a root of all kinds of evil, for which some have strayed from the faith in their greediness and pierced themselves with many sorrows"*

115

1 Timothy 6: 9 – 10. Stripped of her wealth she will be seen to be what she is, empty. Her prosperity hides the corruption of her nature that is now revealed. She thought that she could live independently from God, but demons and all that is detestable take the space He should have occupied.

"Another angel" Revelation 18: 1 indicates that he was not one of the seven angels who poured out the bowls of wrath, one of whom is showing John this vision (Revelation 17: 1). This judgement is separated in time from the outpouring of wrath.

The call not to be caught up in her sins

We are called to come out of her (verse 4), to live by the standards of the kingdom of heaven not those of the world (Galatians 5: 19 – 26). If we allow ourselves to become caught up in the materialism of the age and craving after wealth, we are in danger of sharing the judgement on this world (Jeremiah 51: 6, 45). Our security must be in God, not in the riches of this world.

The root of Babylon's rebellion is Adam and Eve's sin. They did not trust God to have their best interests at heart. Instead they questioned the truth of what God had told them and decided to go their own way. The essence of Babylon is the assertion of independence from God (Genesis 11:1-4). Man decides to control his own affairs and sort out his own problems. He thinks that he has no need of God.

To come out of her is to live in submission to God, to delight to do the will of the Father, Son and Holy Spirit (1 Timothy 6: 11 – 12). Our desire will be to do what pleases Him. We will have no part in the selfish striving to please only ourselves that characterizes the present age. *"You cannot serve God and mammon"* Matthew 6: 24.

Her pride brings about the fall

Babylon has dispensed with the need for God. As a queen she is independent. Her wealth deceives her into thinking that she is secure from calamity (Isaiah 47: 7). Today, the West enjoys such great wealth that she no longer fears the disasters that afflict mankind (Isaiah 47:8). She has risen above flood, famine and storm. She says I will never go without. Affluence closes minds to God. Living in Babylon it is easy to believe that, in this life, she offers all that God can offer. But it is only in this life and for many, she fails to deliver.

The just retribution

The ten kings will strip Babylon of all her wealth. She has lived only for herself, so now she will be reduced to poverty in proportion to the luxury she once enjoyed (Jeremiah 50: 15, 51:6). She will meet a violent end. The kings burn the harlot with fire (Revelation 17: 16), her downfall will be violent (Isaiah 47: 11). Her downfall will also be swift (Isaiah 47: 9, Jeremiah 51: 8). As the center of the World economy global trade will be ruined by her fall. All the nations of the world will be affected and mourn her downfall, especially those who grew rich through her. It is probable that the *'in one hour'*, not only emphasizes the swiftness of her downfall, it also corresponds to the period in which the ten kings assert their power.

The world is in despair. But the saints are called to rejoice (Revelation 18: 20). Those committed to Babylon have lost everything. The saints who, *'come out of her'*, have their treasure stored in heaven. There it cannot be lost (Matthew 6: 19 – 20).

The kingdom of the beast is still to come. The saints know that this will be short lived and soon dispensed with. Soon, the Kingdom of Christ, in which the saints have laid up their treasure, will be established.

The fall of the kingdom of this world is the second warning to men to repent before the outpouring of the wrath of God. Jesus said that this would be a time for the saints to rejoice (Luke 21: 28). The rejoicing of the saints contrasts to the misery of the merchants, whose wealth is laid up on earth.

Never to rise again

Never again will God allow a rebellious empire such as Babylon to arise. She stood against all who were faithful to God. In her downfall God is judging all the kingdoms of this world through the entire span of history.

Note: The name Babylon means 'confusion'. This prophecy in Revelation 17 and 18, has caused much confusion due to the limiting of its application to false religion. At the time of the Reformation and for the next 300 years, the Protestant Church almost without exception, applied the prophecy to the Roman Catholic Church as it embodied a corrupted form of Christianity. But Babylon, although the source of false religion, is much more. As has been noted, at the time of her downfall she is seen as an economic power preoccupied with the acquisition of wealth. She is proud of her independence from God. She is best understood as all that Mankind calls "civilisation" and particularly that civilisation which used to be called Christendom. Western / Greek culture is dominant in the present day world.

I believe that in these last days the Western world is the fulfilment of Babylon the Great. As with the church at Laodicea, with its lukewarm veneer of Christianity, God, who is just, will vomit the harlot West out of His mouth.

EL EMET

THE GOD OF TRUTH

Translated as 'God of Truth' in Psalm 32: 5. '*Emet*' also means firmness and faithfulness. God is faithful to His promises. He will come again to take us to the place prepared for us. *"These are the true sayings of God."* Revelation 19: 9. He cannot lie.

REFERENCE	TOPIC	TIMESPAN
Revelation 19: 1–10	The Son of God claims His bride.	The beginning of the 1,000 years reign of Christ on earth.

Babylon the Great, the kingdom of this world, has been overthrown plunging the world into a period of economic chaos and a breakdown of society. How are we to respond to the terrible times and persecution which follow the fall of Babylon? Revelation 18:20 calls on us to rejoice! We rejoice because the kingdom of this world has received its long deserved judgment. A judgment held back due to the longsuffering nature of God.

We will rejoice for, as Jesus has assured us, *"when these things begin to happen, look up and lift up your heads because your redemption draws near."* Luke 21: 28. Men's hearts will fail from fear of what is coming on the earth. But those who know their God will be confident that soon they will see their King.

For a brief period of time the vacuum left by Babylon's fall is filled by the final empire of the beast. Mankind instead of turning to God will receive Satan's man as their saviour. Men will persecute those who remain faithful to Christ. But we will still rejoice because Jesus has promised that for our sakes the time will be cut short.

Jesus is now revealed, as the One who makes His people ready to be united with Him forever.

Christ and His bride

Revelation 19: 1 - 10

This rejoicing is taken up in heaven with a fourfold *Alleluia*. Alleluia is from two Hebrew words meaning 'Praise the Lord'.

First, the multitude cry out, *"Alleluia, Salvation and glory and honour and power belong to the Lord our God"*. Revelation 19:1. It is the same salvation theme that the vast multitude of the saved sing when standing before the throne after the sixth seal is opened. (Revelation 7: 12). God is praised for the justice of His judgment which has avenged the blood of His servants.

Again the multitude cry *Alleluia* in response to the judgment which has fallen on Babylon. Her smoke rises for ever. Never again will there be a kingdom of this world in opposition to God. The elders and Living creatures echo this praise with the words *"Amen! Alleluia!"* Amen means truth. All that the multitude say is true. The Lord our God is worthy.

The praise concludes with *"Alleluia! For the Lord God Omnipotent reigns!"* Omnipotent means all powerful. He is truly King of Kings and Lord of Lords.

When the fifth seal was opened we heard the cry of the martyrs, *"How long, O Lord, holy and true, until you judge and avenge our blood on those who dwell on the earth?"* Revelation 6: 10. Their prayer has now been answered. God has judged the Harlot. The battle between the kingdoms is over. The number of their fellow servants, who did not love their lives even to the death, is now complete.

The Marriage of the Lamb

Now there are other things to occupy our minds. It is a time of celebration for all those who fear God. The wedding feast has come. This is a marriage made in heaven but celebrated on earth.

Long ago the Lord declared that Israel was His bride. *"For your Husband is your maker"* Isaiah 54:5. The Lord added in Isaiah 54: 7,

"For a mere moment I have forsaken you, but with great mercies I will gather you". When the Lord restores Israel as His bride she will never again be forsaken. There will come a time when the Lord will betroth Israel to, *"Me forever".* Hosea 2: 19.

Israel is and will remain the bride of Christ. We as Gentiles are grafted in to the root stock of Israel. (Romans 11: 17 - 18). Paul stresses this to ensure that we, the Gentiles, do not become arrogant toward Israel. It is their blessings, which by grace, we share. The Lord has made it possible for us to benefit from their inheritance.

A day is coming when the Lord will restore Israel. On that day the believing Jews, the Gentile church and the now repentant nation of Israel will be united as one. (Ephesians 2: 14).

Paul is jealous for the Corinthian congregation that they may be presented to Jesus as a pure chaste virgin. (2 Corinthians 11:2). He understood that sharing in the same rootstock as Israel, the Gentiles would one day receive the same blessing. To be fit for the Bridegroom they must be pure and holy.

The Jewish Wedding

It was the custom in the Jewish wedding that after the betrothal, the bridegroom would return home to prepare a place for his bride. While he was away the bride would spend her time preparing her wedding clothes. She would make a beautifully embroidered garment to wear. When the betrothal time is completed she would be dressed and ready to go out to meet the Bridegroom. The home would be a buzz of excitement and anticipation. The bride's attendants would keep going to the windows to see if there was any sign of the bridegroom coming. This is to be the bride's special day when all will see her in her beauty and share in her joy.

How do we ensure that, on that day, like the Jewish bride, we have a wedding garment fit for the Bridegroom? Two things are said about the wedding garments.

Firstly the Bride is *"granted to be arrayed in fine linen clean and bright."* Revelation 19:8. These garments are a gift from the Bridegroom. In Corinthians we read that: *"For He made Him who knew no sin to become sin for us, that we might become the righteousness of God in Him."* 2 Corinthians 5: 21. Jesus has taken our sin stained garments and paid the cost of having them cleaned. It is not by right that the Bride wears her wedding clothes but by grace.

Secondly these garments are, *"the righteous acts of the saints."* Our righteous acts are the outworking of our faith. They are all the actions done in obedience to Christ. The garments are Christ's gift to us, secured by His sacrifice on the cross. The embroidery is our response. The importance of the words, *"Blessed are the ones who are called to the marriage supper of the Lamb"*, are underlined by the statement *"These are the true words of God"*.

Jesus told several parables warning of the danger of failing to enter the wedding feast. There was the servant who beat his fellow slaves, followed by the ten virgins, five of whom did not have sufficient oil, and then the servant who buried his talent. The evil servant is punished and assigned a place with the hypocrites. The foolish virgins are not recognized and the lazy servant is consigned to outer most darkness. (Matthew 24: 45 – 51, 25:1-30).

In another parable Jesus likens His return to a wedding feast. (Matthew 22: 1 – 14). At that feast one man was found without a wedding garment. He is bound hand and foot and cast into the outer darkness. The man clearly expected to be welcomed to the feast for he is speechless when challenged by the Lord as to how he entered the feast without a garment. At another time Jesus warned that many will expect to be admitted into the kingdom of heaven. They will say to Him *"Lord, Lord"*. He will respond that He never knew them. (Matthew 7: 21 – 23). In his letter James wrote that *"faith without works is dead."* James 2: 26. True faith will bear fruit in a person's life.

Christians need to ensure that on that day we are worthy to be clothed in fine linen bright and clean or we will miss out on the blessing. Are we embroidering the clean linen garment which Jesus has given us with righteous acts carried out in obedience and love for our Lord?

The Wedding

When Israel is restored, the Lord will spread a canopy over mount Zion (Isaiah 4:5). The word is, 'Huppah', referring to the wedding canopy which is spread over the bride and bridegroom at the marriage ceremony.

The raptured church, clothed in fine garments, is to return with Christ to Jerusalem. In Jerusalem the church will be united with a now repentant nation of Israel (Zechariah 12:10) to become the bride of Christ.

Worship only God

When John saw the scroll, which no one could open, he wept. (Revelation 5: 4). He now sees the fulfilment of all he longs for. His reaction is to fall down in worship of the one who brings the good news (Revelation 19: 10). The angel commands him not to worship him, as he is only a fellow servant. When tempted by the devil in the wilderness Jesus declared that God alone is worthy of worship (Luke 4: 8).

There is no greater blessing than being invited to *"the marriage supper of the Lamb."* But how many are preparing for that day? The Jewish bride spent her year of betrothal in preparation for the wedding day. She wanted to look radiant for her bridegroom. A bride in which He could be proud.

Jesus is coming for a bride. Are we getting ready?

REVELATIONS OF JESUS CHRIST

EL GIBBOR
THE MIGHTY GOD

One of the titles given to Jesus in Isaiah 9: 6 is *'Mighty God'*. On his return Jesus will be revealed to the world as the 'Mighty God'. No more the suffering servant, now He is **King of Kings and Lord of Lords.**

REFERENCE	TOPIC	TIMESPAN
Revelation 19:11 to Revelation 20:3	We now see Jesus as He really is, the mighty Son of God.	One day soon when Jesus returns.

What will Jesus be like when he appears to claim the kingdom of this world for His own? For a time Jesus humbled Himself and lived among men. Of Himself He was able to say *"for I am gentle and lowly in heart."* Matthew 11: 29. In Philippians 2: 7 we read *"but made Himself of no reputation, taking the form of a bond servant, and coming in the likeness of men."* It is a great mystery how the Creator of the universe and everything which lives, could become a man. But as we commented in the first chapter, that is all history. In that chapter we were introduced to Jesus as He now is in heaven. He is radiant with eyes of fire. No more the meek servant, He is now the glorified Son of God.

"But we see Jesus, who was made a little lower than the angels, for the suffering of death, crowned with glory and honour, .." Hebrews 2:9. When we see Jesus it will be as a conquering king. He is the Mighty One before whom all creation trembles.

Christ the Conqueror
Revelation 19: 11 – 20: 3

When the first seal was opened it revealed a rider on a white horse. He represented man's efforts to rule this earth independently from God. Man's efforts will culminate in the reign of the Antichrist. We now see Christ, the Son of Man, who will bring the rule of God to the whole earth. He is the only man who can hold the reins of world power and ensure peace, justice and blessing for all mankind. (Isaiah 9: 6-7, 11: 4-5, 42: 1 – 4). Jesus comes in power to judge the wicked and to set up a kingdom that will last forever. His names portray His character, integrity and authority. (Ps 96:10-13).

Faithful and true

In contrast to all the lies and deceit of Babylon, the Beast and the false prophet, He is faithful to His promises, never failing those who trust Him. He is the truth, which evil men have denied, choosing the lies of Satan in its place. (Isaiah 11:5, John 7:18, Hebrews 3: 2-6). He can judge in righteousness because He is righteous in all His ways. He makes war to overcome mankind's rebellion and establish His kingdom. Eyes of fire remind us that when we see Him, He will be as revealed in the first chapter of Revelation, nothing is hidden from His sight. His many crowns confirm that He has been given authority over many nations. All that Satan once promised to Jesus, if He would bow down to him, is now His by right.

A name no one can know.

His name is a secret between Him and His Father. It is so special that it is hidden from men and angels. There is an unsearchable intimacy in the deity which none of His creation can understand or share.

Blood stained garments

> *"Who is this who comes from Edom,*
> *With dyed garments from Bozrah,*
> *This One who is glorious in His apparel*
> *Travelling in the greatness of His strength?*
> *"I who speak in righteousness, mighty to save."*
> *Why is Your apparel red,*
> *And Your garments like one who treads in the winepress?*
> *"I have trodden the winepress alone,*
> *And from the peoples no one was with Me.*

126

For I have trodden them in My anger,
And trampled them in My fury;
Their blood is sprinkled upon My garments,
And I have stained all My robes.
For the day of vengeance is in My heart,
And the year of My redeemed has come.
I looked, but there was no one to help,
And I wondered
That there was no one to uphold;
Therefore My own arm brought salvation for Me;
And My own fury, it sustained Me.
I have trodden down the peoples in My anger,
Made them drunk in My fury,
And brought down their strength to the earth."

Isaiah 63: 1 – 6

When the sixth seal is opened the people of this world try to hide in fear. They cry out to the mountains to fall on them to hide them from the One who sits on the throne *"For the great day of His wrath has come,"* (Revelation 6: 17).

In fury Jesus will trample the nations and bring judgment on an evil world. This is the day of vengeance of God. *"'Vengeance is mine, I will repay', says the Lord. And again 'The Lord will judge His people'. It is a fearful thing to fall into the hands of the living God."* Hebrews 10: 30 - 31.

Jesus shed His own blood to purchase men form out of this world (Ephesians 1: 7– 10). He alone brought salvation and after the Father's wrath, Jesus will bring retribution.

Word of God

The Word of God, is used by John in his gospel and first letter. It is the energising Word of power that spoke worlds into being and healed the blind and lame. (John 1:1, 1 John 1:1).

The armies of heaven

The living and the dead in Christ have been gathered up to meet Jesus in the air. (1 Thessalonians 4: 16 - 17). They have been transformed receiving new bodies. Clothed in white they come prepared to join with Jesus at the wedding feast. Before that joyful occasion they return with Him to witness His victory.

The Sword and the Rod.

To exercise His rule on earth Jesus brings two weapons. *"The sword of the Spirit which is the word of God."* Ephesians 6: 17. *"For the word of God is living and powerful, sharper than any two edged sword, piercing even to the division of soul and spirit, and of joints and marrow, and is a discerner of the thoughts and intents of the heart."* Hebrews 4: 12. With this sword Jesus will reveal secret thoughts. Nothing can be hidden from Him. He will rule in righteousness for all His judgments will be perfect.

His rule will be firm. He will break the nations *"with a rod of iron"*. Psalm 2: 9. This is not yet the perfect world of the new heavens and the earth. It is the old rebellious world under the benign but firm rule of Jesus Christ.

KING OF KINGS AND LORD OF LORDS

He is Lord of heaven and earth. He comes not in meekness, but power. Once he entered Jerusalem, on a donkey, and was rejected by His own people. Now He comes as conqueror, riding on a white horse, to be accepted as King. He will be above all rulers and authorities.

The Feast of Creation

The call of the angel precedes the coming battle. The defeat of the armies of this world is certain. With the revealing of the sons of God, all creation is set free from its slavery to corruption (Romans 8: 19 – 21). Creation will be renewed and share in the freedom of the children of God (Isaiah 11: 6 – 9). A grim terrible picture follows, which may offend. The natural world, which has suffered so long from man's sin, is invited to celebrate its being rid of those who have caused so much destruction. This is a reference back to Ezekiel 39:17 – 20 where it is called a sacrificial meal. The birds and beasts are invited to feast on the remains of the armies of the beast.

Armageddon

This day when the nations are gathered for judgement was foreseen by *Isaiah, Joel* and *Zechariah* hundreds of years earlier. In Isaiah it is *the day of the Lord's vengeance.* (Isaiah 34: 8). Joel describes it as *a day of judgment.* (Joel 3: 12). In Zechariah it is *the day when the Lord fights in defence of Jerusalem,* (Zechariah 14: 1-3). Although Satan stirs up the nations of the world, it is God who gathers them. The whole world is united in its rejection of the King of Israel.

Ezekiel 39 provides a more detailed prophecy of this time when the nations of the world are gathered against Israel. It is set in the time when God restores the fortunes of Israel. Little detail of the battle is given, presumably because it is not a battle. The enemies of Christ are slain by the sword which comes from His mouth. The Creator of the universe merely has to say the word and the armies are crushed. The Lord will judge all flesh by fire and His sword (Isaiah 66: 16).

In punishment for deceiving the world, the beast and the false prophet are thrown into the lake of fire. No one else is sent there at this time. The beast came from the abyss and therefore he will not be returned to that place. Already raised from the dead the beast has received a new body. In that body he will suffer extreme torment.

Satan bound

The names of Satan describe his character. *The dragon* is fierce, *the serpent,* subtle, *the devil* means, *'accuser'* and Satan means, *'adversary'.* Above all, he is a deceiver. To complete the victory, and prepare the way for the reign of Christ, Satan is bound and imprisoned for 1000 years. He will not be allowed to trouble the world during the reign of Christ.

He is not consigned to the lake of fire because God has plans to use him one more time.

REVELATIONS OF JESUS CHRIST

BEN ELOHIM
THE SON OF GOD

"Yet I have set My King on My holy hill Zion." Psalm 2: 6. As we read on we discover that the king is His Son, who we now know to be Jesus the Messiah. The nations may rage but He will reign.

REFERENCE	TOPIC	TIMESPAN
Revelation 20: 4–9	The millenial reign of Christ.	The close of the Church Age and the next 1,000 years.

Before Jesus ascended to heaven the disciples asked Him, *"Lord, will You at this time restore the kingdom to Israel?"* Acts 1: 6. Jesus did not answer their question. Instead He directed their thoughts to the task in hand. Their task was, in the power of the Holy Spirit, to be witnesses to Jesus throughout the earth.

He did not deny that a time would come, as prophesied in the Old Testament, when the Messiah would reign over all the earth. The timing of that reign, as with the timing of His return, was hidden with His Father.

Revelation opens with the words *"The revelation of Jesus Christ, which God gave Him"*. This revelation comes from the Father. We now have the answer to the disciples' question. The Father has set the context in which the reign of His beloved Son will be established.

Christ the King
Revelation 20: 4 - 9

When the angel *Gabriel* appeared to *Mary* to tell her that she was to bear a child, he announced that, *"the Lord God will give Him the throne of His father David."* Luke 1: 32. We now see Jesus the Christ coming to claim that throne.

The kingdom of this world has fallen. The reign of the beast overthrown. Satan has been banished. The stage is set for the greatest coronation in history. All the crowns and all the symbols of authority of all the nations will be handed over to Him.

The reign of the Saints

When we are caught up to be with Jesus from that time onwards we will always be with Him (1 Thessalonians 4: 17). When He comes back to reign we also come back to reign with Him. "And I saw thrones and they sat on them and judgment was committed to them." Revelation 20:4.

Who is sitting on the thrones?

The answer from scripture is that all the saints are seated on thrones. The faithful in the church at Laodicea are promised that if they overcome, they will sit with Jesus on His throne. At Thyatira, the overcomers are told that they will have power over the nations. In the vision of eternity the elders and living creatures sing a new song. The redeemed will be kings and priests, and will reign on the earth (Revelation 5: 9 – 10). In the prophecies of Daniel it says that after a period of testing, the dominion will be handed to the saints of the Most High (Daniel 7: 27). The Corinthian church was scolded for taking one another to court when they should be preparing to judge this world (1 Corinthians 6: 1 – 2). Paul reminds Timothy that if we endure with Him we shall also reign with Him (2 Timothy 2: 12). It is the faithful church which is seated on the thrones, sharing in Christ's rule.

Special mention is then made of the martyrs who died during the reign of the beast. For their comfort, those who gave up their lives, are assured that they will live again to reign with Christ. They stood against the evil of Satan's empire. Now they will be part of Jesus Christ's administration which will rule the world.

Saints and martyrs will each be given responsibilities in the kingdom. Those who have used their talents well, in this present age, will be given greater responsibility in this kingdom (Luke 19:12-27).

The Millennium

This passage in Revelation says that the reign of Christ will last 1000 years. The term 'millennium' comes from the Latin *'mille'* which means *'thousand'* and *'annus'* which means *'year'*. Numerous Old Testament prophecies describe this time when the Lord will reign. This is the only place in the Bible which sets a time limit on that reign.

The prophet *Habakkuk* foresaw this time. *"For the earth will be filled with the knowledge of the glory of the Lord, as the waters cover the sea."* Habakkuk 2: 14. Jesus will reign over all the earth. Psalm 72 provides more detail of that reign. Isaiah sees a time of universal peace, (Isaiah 2: 4) and a time when the earth will be restored to its created harmony, (Isaiah 11: 6 – 9). Jesus will judge the earth with righteousness, (Isaiah 11: 4) and there will be abundance of crops (Amos 9:13).

For 1000 years this world will be under the benevolent rule of Christ. Peace and prosperity such as it has not known since the days before the fall. But Christ will have to rule with a rod of iron. (Psalm 2: 8, 9, Revelation 2: 26, 27, Revelation 12: 5). Anything that is contrary to the laws of God will be suppressed. Not all will rejoice at having to live under this benign but strict rule.

At the end of the 1000 years Satan is allowed to tempt mankind one last time. He will taunt men as he did *Eve* in Eden: *'Do you really want this man to rule over you?'* Look at all the restrictions He places on your lives'. 'You would be so much better off if I ruled over you'.

The Bible teaches that after living for 1000 years in a perfect world under the benign but firm rule of Christ, people rebel. They will seek to throw off His reign.

The gospel of the street is; *'if there is a heaven I will be alright for I am a good person'*. By implication, if God doesn't allow *'good people'* into heaven He is unjust.

Rev 20: 4 - 10 demonstrates the absolute justice of Christ, in banishing even those who appear righteous in the eyes of the world, from His New Jerusalem. To explain this we will look at two widely debated passages.

The Sheep and the Goats

At the end of this present age there will be a judgment (Matthew 25: 31 – 46). This is not the final judgement. The judgment is described in a parable which identifies three groups of people: the *'Sheep'*, who are selected because they showed compassion to 'My brethren', the *'Goats'*, who are rejected because they had no compassion, and 'My Brethren'. Elsewhere Jesus defined His brethren as *"those who hear the word of God and do it"*. Luke 8: 21. At this point in time the followers of Christ have been raptured (1 Thessalonians 4: 17), received a new body (1 Corinthians 15: 52) and returned with Christ to earth. These followers of Christ are *His brethren.* They were separated out at the rapture and now return to form the third group.

This parable is about who will populate the Millennial Kingdom. The sheep will be divided from the goats. The sheep are to; *"inherit the kingdom prepared for you from the foundation of the world."* The reward is based on their good works. Even a small act of mercy gains them entry into this kingdom. But that is contrary to the rest of scripture which teaches that salvation is by faith.

From the foundation of the world it was the intention of the Father to establish a kingdom ruled over by His beloved Son (Ephesians 1: 3 -14). Therefore it can be said of this kingdom that it was prepared before the foundation of the world. The sheep are blessed because the Father has shown them mercy. They will be allowed to experience a world ruled over by Jesus Christ. The sheep are the 'good' people of this world, compassionate and kind, but not believers. If the sheep had trusted the Lord before His return, they would have been counted among His brethren and already separated out.

This is not a second chance. Their lives have not ended. It is the 'good' people who will make up the nations which populate the planet during the reign of Christ. I do not know how many of those who will live in the millennial kingdom will gladly accept the reign of Christ and enter into a saving relationship with their Lord. What seems apparent is that most will resent His rule.

The fate of the goats, who showed no mercy, is to share Satan's punishment in the everlasting fire. I believe that the goats are the same as the people who took the mark of the beast. Their torment is described in Revelation 14: 10 - 11.

The final rebellion

We move on to the final outcome of that reign which vindicates the justice of God. In Ezekiel chapters 38 and 39 there is a description of the time when *Gog* and his hordes come up to attack Israel. A number of views have been put forward with regard to the timing of this invasion. The main ones are Pre-tribulation, Mid-tribulation, Post-tribulation, the beginning of the Millennium and the end of the Millennium.

To those views I add another understanding. Two events are described in these chapters. The events are similar but have some marked differences to set them apart in time. The separate events tie in with Revelation 19 and 20.

In Revelation 19 there is an allusion to Ezekiel 39. The birds are gathered to the supper of the great God. It is the final rebellion against Christ coming to reign on the earth.

Revelation 20: 8 makes a more direct reference to *Gog* and *Magog* as in Ezekiel 38.

At the end of this present age when Jesus returns to claim His throne the people of this world will reject His rule and gather to fight against Him. Following the victory of Christ, all the wicked are removed. (Matt 13: 41). The population of the world, during the reign of Christ,

135

will be made up of two peoples; Christ's brethren who have proved their loyalty and faithfulness, and the sheep who are, as we have seen, made up of 'good' people.

At the end of the 1000 years the sheep are given a choice. Satan is released to test them. At last they have a champion to stand against Christ. The 'good' people and their descendants will reject the reign of Christ. His laws have been a burden to them.

That is why we have these two descriptions of the rebellion by Gog. The end of the coming age will be almost identical to the end of this present age. Both ages will end with a rebellion as mankind resists the reign of Christ.

The reign of Christ proves that even the 'good people', in reality, hate His rule. All excuses that man makes as to why he disobeys God have now been answered.

The citizens of the millennial kingdom and all those who preceded them in the former ages, have one thing in common, *"they love and practice a lie"*. The same old lie that *Eve* fell for in the garden. It is Satan's constant lie that God does not want to give the best to His creation. Satan taunts, *"listen to me and you will become like God"*.

Such is the deceitfulness of man's heart, the number of those who are stirred by Satan to rebel is like the sand on the sea shore. They have experienced the reign of Christ and seen this world returned to its former paradise. Yet despite the benevolent reign of Christ they will not submit to Him. Instead they listen to Satan.

For a time men lived in a foretaste of the perfect kingdom of God. Their one wish was to destroy it. It is the perfect justice of God that only those who freely chose to submit to His rule over their lives, can enter through the gates to the eternal city.

Those who are outwardly good by the standards of this world but inwardly in rebellion cannot and never will be able to enter.

The judgment of Jesus has been vindicated.

He is righteous and just. Worthy is the Lamb.

EL DEOT
THE GOD OF KNOWLEDGE

Hannah rejoiced because God knew and answered the silent prayers of her heart, (1 Sam 2: 3). God has perfect knowledge of all things from beginning to end. He is Omniscient, knowing both our prayers and worship and also those thoughts which we wish to keep hidden.

REFERENCE	TOPIC	TIMESPAN
Revelation 20: 10–15	The final judgement of all who have ever lived.	Beginning of Eternity.

Will all be forgiven in the end?

The Bible divides people into two categories. *"He who believes in Him [Jesus] is not condemned; but he who does not believe is condemned already because he has not believed in the name of the only begotten Son of God."* John 3: 18.

We either believe and trust Jesus or we reject Him. It really is as simple as that. Mankind fell because *Eve* believed Satan rather than God. It is the glory of God that salvation is based on a simple question; *'Do you believe in Jesus Christ?'*

Sadly many will not believe in Jesus Christ. The ending of the millennial reign of Christ confirms mankind's deep rooted hatred of God. The justice of God has been vindicated by the rebellion at the end of the millennial reign of Christ. Even after having lived in the kingdom ruled by Christ the people want none of it. Their one wish is to destroy it, so they rebel. It is the perfect justice of God that only those who freely chose to submit to His rule over their lives, can enter through the gates to the eternal city.

With that in mind we ask the question, *what is God to do with all those who refuse His way of escape?*

Christ the Judge

Revelation 20: 10 - 15

Satan has served his purpose. He has been used to demonstrate that there is only one solution to sin. Even living in paradise will not cure it. In the end, mankind is no different to Adam and Eve. Despite the tragic history of this world, people are still prepared to listen to the lies of the one who says that God does not really want the best for them. That is why the new heavens and new earth can only be peopled by those who have willingly turned their backs on disobedience and submitted to a loving Saviour. The only cure for sin is repentance. True heart felt sorrow over the grief we have caused the Father and a desire to live a life pleasing to him. Without repentance the grip sin has on us cannot be broken.

Satan was the cause of mankind's fall. As the result of his deception, billions have had their lives destroyed. He has constantly stirred up hatred between men, and against God. His guilt has been evident from the beginning. There is no need of a trial, He is cast into the lake of fire where he joins the beast and false prophet. They have already been tormented for 1000 years. The divine verdict: their punishment is to continue in torment day and night for ever and ever.

The Throne

The time of judgment for all who have ever lived has come. A great white throne is set up. We read that the earth and heaven flee away from before the face of Him who sits on the throne.

Before the judgment takes place the old order is removed. *"But the day of the Lord will come as a thief in the night, in which the heavens will pass away with a great noise, and the elements will melt with fervent heat; both the earth and the works that are in it will be burned up."* 2 Peter 3:10. Despite the reign of Christ this world has been so polluted by sin that God has to destroy it and start again. Everything sinful is burnt up and destroyed.

The throne is set up but who is the *"Him who sat on it"*? verse 11.

Jesus answered that question, *"For the Father judges no one, but has committed all judgment to the Son."* John 5: 22. The Father delegates the judgment of men to a man, His Son.

The Judgment

A time will come when everyone will stand before the judgment seat of Christ. No one who has ever lived can escape that day. This is the day of final reckoning which none can avoid. It is a day of absolute justice. Unlike our own courts of law, which make judgments based on imperfect evidence, in this court everything is known. It is all written in the books. Nothing can be hidden, not even our secret thoughts, all will be made public (Luke 12: 2 – 3). Those who trusted in the pomp and glory of this world will find that it comes to nothing.

Everyone standing before the throne is judged by the things written in the scrolls. The evidence there convicts them for, *"there is none who is righteous, not even one,"* Romans 3: 10. The destiny of the wicked is to join the devil in the lake of fire. A destiny so terrible that Jesus suffered extreme agony and immeasurable torment in the separation from His Father, so that we need not go there. Hell must be very terrible, for Him to go through all that, so that we could be spared.

In the end our sin is not the problem. Sin does not condemn us for Christ has atoned for it on the cross. It is rejection of the gift of life received by faith in Jesus, the one and only source of life (John 3: 14 -21). Refusal to believe in Jesus will condemn us to the lake of fire.

Those who have never heard

At this point some will protest, *"What about those who have never heard?"* They cannot respond to someone about whom they know nothing! This is a difficult question with which many struggle and others chose to remain agnostic.

In the introduction to his Gospel, John presents Jesus as the light of the world. Then in chapter 3 we read *"And this is the condemnation that the light has come into the world and men love darkness rather than light because their deeds were evil. For everyone practicing evil hates the light and does not come to the light, lest his deeds be exposed. But he who does the truth comes to the light, that his deeds may be clearly seen, that they have been done in God."* The harsh biblical view of man is that we are all sinners who love the darkness rather than the light (Romans 1: 18 – 23). In hiding from the light we reject the One who is the light. Can we respond to the light if we have never heard of Jesus? If we can answer that question it will tell us what happens to those who have never heard. Our responsibility is to make sure that the number who have never heard is as few as possible. But whatever happens God is just in all his judgments.

The redeemed

What about those who were part of the first resurrection? They have lived with Christ during His reign for a thousand years. Will they also be judged? I believe that the redeemed will also be judged on that day. For them there is no fear. If we are part of the first resurrection the second death will have no power over us (Revelation 20: 6). On that day we will be judged according to our deeds (2 Corinthians 5: 10). Our work will be tested in the fire. If it endures we will be rewarded (1 Corinthians 3: 13). If consumed by the fire we will still enter the New Jerusalem but without any reward. In this present time we are encouraged to lay up our treasure in heaven ready for that day (Matthew 6: 20). It is the best investment we can ever make.

Everlasting Conscious Torment?

Many are troubled by a widely held belief that the torment of the wicked will continue for ever and ever without any relief. I believe that this idea comes from Greek thinking and is not founded on the Bible. The Greeks believed that the soul was indestructible and would continue to exist once set free from the body. Therefore if the wicked are condemned to torment in the lake of fire, it follows that their torment will continue for ever. The Greek idea of the indestructible soul and everlasting torment, entered the church through *Tertullian*. Later it was consolidated by *Augustine of Hippo* and became a doctrine of the Roman Catholic Church. The Bible does not teach that the soul is indestructible. Jesus said, *"Do not fear those who kill the body but cannot kill the soul. But rather fear Him who is able to destroy both soul and body in Gehenna."* Matthew 10: 28. In this statement, Jesus corrected the Greek idea of the indestructible soul by saying that God could destroy both body and soul. In contrast to Greek thinking the Bible teaches that all existence is in God. *"And He is before all things, and in Him all things consist."* Colossians 1: 17. *"upholding all things by the word of His power,"* Hebrews 1: 3 and *"In Him we live and move and have our being,"* Acts 17: 28. Cut off from the sustaining power of Christ the wicked will cease to exist. *"All things were made through Him, and without Him nothing was made that was made. In Him was life and the life was the light of men."* John 1: 3, 4. Jesus warned of the danger of being cast into the *"outer darkness; there would be weeping and gnashing of teeth."* (Matthew 8: 12, 22: 13, 25: 30), He was surely describing a place outside of His sustaining power and light. This is confirmed in 2 Thessalonians 1: 9 *"These shall be punished with everlasting destruction from the presence of the Lord and the glory of His power."* It is also confirmed in Revelation 14: 10, *"he shall also drink the wine of the wrath of God, which is poured out full strength into the cup of His indignation. He shall be tormented with fire and brimstone in the presence of the holy angels and in the presence of the Lamb."* This passage describes the punishment which falls on those who accept the mark of the beast. But note, this punishment is carried out while those who have become the enemies of Christ are still in His presence and therefore within *"the glory of His power."* I know that this is controversial for some but, from my own studies, I have concluded that there is no scripture which, when understood in context, specifically states that everyone will suffer everlasting torment. The above verse from Revelation 14, continues *"And the smoke of their torment ascends for ever and ever; and they will have no rest day or night, who worship the beast and his image, and who ever receives the mark of his name."* Revelation 14: 11. The force of this passage lies in it being an extreme punishment for a particular group of people. It loses its impact if it is applied to everyone. The New Testament consistently teaches, both in words and imagery, that the general end of sinful man is destruction (Matthew 7: 13). The thought that the torment may not last for ever, must not be allowed in any way to reduce the terror of hell and the need to warn people of this terrible destiny. The lake of fire is final. It is everlasting in the sense that there is no going back. Those who are condemned to that place face the prospect of punishment, torment and destruction. But whatever the duration, Jesus is absolutely just. All present at the judgment will witness that God has acted with perfect righteousness and mercy.

IMMANUEL
GOD WITH US

Isaiah prophesied that the Son born to the virgin would be called *'Immanuel'*, (Isaiah 7: 14). *Immanuel* means *'God with us'*. The prophecy was fulfilled by the birth of Jesus the Messiah. The closing words of Revelation reveal that there is a greater fulfilment to come. Both the Father and the Son will come and dwell in their creation. We will serve Him and reign in that creation forever and ever.

REFERENCE	TOPIC	TIMESPAN
Revelation 21 and 22	Looks to eternity and completes the vision.	Eternity.

Is this the end? The first time a person reads through the Bible from cover to cover, coming to the closing chapters of Revelation feels like quite an achievement. The Bible contains an epic story stretching from before time began to beyond the distant future.

We now come to the end of one story and the beginning of another. The story which is ending is the one which started long ago in Genesis. In the beginning God created a perfect world and gave it to mankind to look after. Soon Satan entered that world. In jealousy he deceived *Eve* causing her to disobey God. The fall of man soon corrupted the whole of creation. The Bible recounts that story as it leads through the history of a chosen nation up to the pivotal event of history, the life, death and resurrection of Jesus Christ. In Jesus, we who deserve punishment for our sin can, through faith, be forgiven.

But now it is revealed that this is not the end. It is only the prologue to the real story. The final two chapters of Revelation provide us with a trailer for what is to come.

The close of Revelation is a description of the fulfilment of all that

God intended when He created man. It is a description in words using things we know.

That is the only means of revealing to us what, *""Eye has not seen, nor ear heard, nor have entered the heart of man the things which God has prepared for those who love Him", but God has revealed them to us through His Spirit."* 1 Corinthians 2: 9 – 10. We should let the Holy Spirit use these words to thrill our imagination with the glory of all that God is doing and of which we can be a part.

Christ and His Bride

Revelation 21: 1 – 8

The old creation has fled away from the presence of God. Everything sinful and evil has been cast into the lake of fire. The devil and his followers will never again disturb the peace of heaven.

The Son of God left the glory of His Father's house, emptied Himself and became Man (Philippians 2: 5 – 11) so that He would win a bride and bring her to a new home, which is the new earth. That bride is now seen. The faithful have been prepared by the Holy Spirit to be that bride. They will live with the Bridegroom in the place prepared for them, the New Jerusalem. God and men will live forever in harmony. The lessons of sin have been learnt. Death, sorrow and pain are now things of the past. Even in glory Jesus has not changed. The One who washed the disciple's feet will wipe away our tears. He will wipe away all the sorrowful memories of the past. In His presence, due to His love and wisdom, we will have eternal joy and peace.

"as a bride adorned for her husband."

After the betrothal period the Jewish bridegroom would go to collect his bride and bring her to the home he has prepared for her. I can imagine that home decorated by the bridegroom ready for the wedding day and receiving his bride. The bridegroom would want the new home to look resplendent to welcome his bride.

In this heavenly wedding; it is the Bridegroom who provides the wedding garments for His Bride. (Revelation 19: 7, 8). It is the Bridegroom who comes for and places the Bride in her new home. (1 Thessalonians 4: 16, 17). It is the Bridegroom who prepares this wonderful home for His Bride. (John 14: 2, 3).

The Bridegroom will be overjoyed to see His Bride delighting in the splendour of her new home. The New Jerusalem represents the whole of the new heaven and new earth that Jesus has created. '**Adorned**', expresses the idea that like the first creation, it is very good. Only this time there is nothing to spoil it. For Jesus, it is not just the people but the whole new creation in which they dwell, which will be like a bride to Him. He cares for and sustains it all.

The sea

In scripture the organized peoples of the earth are described as *the sea* (Daniel 7: 2 - 3). Divided, turbulent, tossed back and forth by the waves of new ideas and doctrines, without God they are at the mercy of every deceit. Separated into nations whose fortunes, like the tide of the sea, rise and fall. Sometimes there is storm, sometimes calm, but the quest for lasting peace eludes them. John sees that all the turbulence has passed away with the old creation. There is now only one people and real peace reigns.

This is the time for the restitution of all things (Acts 3: 21). It is the time when those searching for a new city will enter the place they longed for (Hebrews 11: 10, 16, 13: 14). There is enough room for everyone.

Only the purified

The work of redemption was completed on the cross when Jesus cried, *"It is finished"* John 19:30. The work of the New Creation will be finished when God proclaims, *"It is done"*. Out of the old has come the new. Paul deals with this principle of death and resurrection (1 Corinthians 15: 36 – 49). The seed is planted and dies, so that a new plant may come from it. This is the principle running through the whole of creation. Without Christ nothing can be made new. *"Therefore if anyone is in Christ, he is a new creation; old things have passed away; behold, all things have become new"* 2 Corinthians 5: 17. God is the *Alpha* and the *Omega*, the *beginning* and the *end*. Everything, which has happened, is happening or will happen, is under His rule.

The new creation

Once the wicked have been dealt with, the full glory of the new creation can be revealed. The creation is so good that God will come to dwell with man. In this new world there will be no more tears, no more death, no more sorrow, no more crying, no more pain. All that spoilt the former world has been destroyed. From His throne God calls us to take special note of the following words for they are faithful and true.

We come back to where the vision started. Jesus who sits on the throne speaks directly to John. *"I am the Alpha and the Omega."* is a repeat of Revelation 1:11. *"It is done."* All that the Father and the Son planned from the beginning is now complete. *"the water of life."* is the drink which will sustain us, while the *'tree of life'* (Revelation 22: 2) will be our food.

"He who overcomes" takes us back to the letters to the seven churches. These are the people who remain faithful despite the apostasy of the church and persecution of the world. All who overcome will be allowed to enter this place prepared for them.

The wicked, defined as those who *"love and practice a lie"*, have been consigned to the lake of fire. Revelation 22: 15 confirms that they have no part in the New Jerusalem. So at the end there will be only two categories of people. *Those who believe the truth* and t*hose who believe the lie.*

Jesus said that *"I am the way the truth and the life."* John 14:6

Satan said that *"you will be like God."* Genesis 3: 5 which is a lie.

In the end it comes down to who do you believe, Jesus or Satan? On that you will be judged.

Revelation 21: 9 – 21

Satan took Jesus to a high mountain to show Him all the kingdoms of the world (Matthew 4: 8 – 10). Jesus saw that He was being offered Babylon, the great prostitute. He refused this tainted bride and was firm in the resolve to purchase a bride who would be glorious and pure.

An angel carries John to a high mountain. From this high mountain John sees that bride radiant in her beauty. *"I will show you the bride the wife of the lamb …….. and showed me the great city the holy Jerusalem descending out of heaven from God."* The glory of God adorns this city. The city and its people are living in harmony with God reconciled through the Son. All the honour, praise and worship is directed towards the Father and the Son.

What did you expect to see? Perhaps as in Revelation 7: 9 – 10 a great multitude praising God? Up to now we have thought of the Bride as the people. Instead we are given a glimpse of the place where the people will live. John would have remembered Jesus' words: *"I go to prepare a place for you."* John14: 2, this is the place which Jesus has prepared.

The walls ensure that all that dwell in the city are secure. The gates with twelve angels guarding them, remind us that when man was ejected from the Garden of Eden, an angel was sent to guard the way to the tree of life. The angels guard the entrances to the city and the way to the tree of life. Eternal life is a precious gift only given to those who receive Jesus. There is no way back from the lake of fire for those who have rejected Christ.

The gates on the East, North, South and West welcome people from the four corners of the earth. The city belongs to the people of God, who are represented by the twelve tribes of Israel whose names are on the gates.

The Apostles were sent out to preach the gospel of Jesus to the whole world. That gospel is the foundation on which the kingdom is built. Only by believing that gospel can we enter the city. Without that faith there is an impenetrable wall, which denies us access to God. The names of the Apostles are on the foundations to remind us that unless we accept the gospel, of which they were witnesses, the wall of separation from God remains.

The proportions of the city and walls are symbolic for perfection. Gold, as pure glass represents something better than the finest man can conceive. The foundations are adorned with precious stones. Precious in the sight of God is the ministry of the Apostles who faithfully bore witness for Him.

After *Judas* betrayed Christ, there were only eleven Apostles. Who does the first of the twelve stones represent? The first foundation is *jasper*, as is the wall. The light of the city is described as like jasper. Christ is her light and her walls are salvation (Isaiah 60:18c, 19). On the breastplate worn by the High Priest the last stone was jasper (Exodus 28: 20). In that foundation we have a memorial to Christ, the first and the last. He was the first apostle and the one foundation of our faith.

A worthless pearl of immense price

Each gate is a single pearl. Jesus described the kingdom of heaven as like *a pearl of great price*. (Matthew 13:46). To the Gentile, at the time of Christ, a pearl was immensely valuable, worth selling everything to buy. But to the Jew a pearl was worthless. It could not be worn because it came from a creature that was unclean.

Why would anyone sell everything to buy an article of no value? The story describes two aspects of the kingdom. To us it is worth everything we have to be part of it. But Jesus sold everything to purchase us who as sinners are worthless. The gates of pearl are an eternal reminder of that infinite sacrifice.

The street of the city is gold, like transparent glass. Everything about this city is transparent. In glory we too will be transparent, by the grace of God we will be transformed so that there will be nothing to hide.

Revelation 21: 22 - 22: 5

We are not transported to live in the spiritual realm. The reverse takes place. The Father and the Son come to dwell in their material creation. Creation becomes the new heaven. Two thousand years ago the eternal Son of God entered our world and became a man. Jesus used the title '*Son of Man*'. He remains a man and will live with us and rule His new creation as a man. When in this vision Jesus revealed Himself to John, it is as the glorified 'Son of Man' (Revelation 1: 13).

In this new creation Jesus will *"transform our lowly body that it may conform to His glorious body"* (Philippians 3: 21). We will receive new bodies in preparation for living in this new creation.

The Light of the Lord

The city will be filled with the presence of God. All earthly aids to worship will no longer be required. There will be fullness of joy and perfect worship in the city.

In this present world our light is merely the light of the sun. Our vision is limited to what can be seen by that light. In heaven we will have the light of God. Everything He sees we will be able to see. In this life most of creation is hidden to us. In the next the vastness of all that God has made will be revealed for us to enjoy.

Isaiah speaks of the glory that God will restore to Zion. It reaches complete fulfilment in the New Jerusalem (Isaiah 60).

The gates are open

The kings of the earth are the ones who will be raised up to reign with Christ (Daniel 7: 27). Back in Revelation 5: 9 – 10 we read a new song which was sung by the Elders and Living Creatures:

"You are worthy to take the scroll,
And open its seals;
For You were slain,
And have redeemed us to God by your blood,
Out of every tribe and tongue and nation,
And made us kings and priests to our God;
And we shall reign on the earth."

In the sight of God the faithful are the true kings of this world. *"And they shall bring the glory and honour of the nations into it"*, is a reminder that the citizens of this city will come out of every nation, tribe, peoples and tongues, (Revelation 7: 9).

The freedom of that city is expressed in the gates never being shut. There is no compulsion because everyone in the city has chosen to follow the Lamb. The night of sin has passed. No one will think of disobedience. All have experienced the consequence of sin. The redeemed are the true glory and honour of any nation for *"righteousness exalts a nation"* Proverbs 14: 34.

Nothing unclean will be allowed to enter the city, only those whose names are written in the Lamb's book of life. We are not to deceive ourselves into thinking that there is any other way to enter the city. It is only by faith in Christ that we can be cleansed and made new, fit to live in the presence of God.

The water of life

The crystal clear water in the river symbolizes the Holy Spirit flowing from the throne of God (John 4: 14). By drinking deeply and often and being baptized in the waters of the river we will be kept clean and pure, fit to live in the transparent radiance of the city. When God created man He breathed His Spirit into him to give life. It is by the power of the Holy Spirit that we will be able to live for ever.

The trees of life nourished by the living water will bear fruit to feed us and leaves to heal us. It creates a wonderful picture of the nations of the world gathered under the shade of the trees, eating the fruit and drinking the water, and living in eternal harmony.

The curse, which divided man from God and man from man, has been removed. In the centre of this wonderful gathering will be the throne of God and of the Lamb. Because we are clean we will be able to look on the face of God and live.

The only reason we are able to be there, is because the Lamb paid the supreme price to redeem us from the punishment that should have been ours. Therefore we shall gladly serve Him and bear His name.

For *Adam* there was not found a suitable companion for him. So God created *Eve*. The Son of Man came seeking a bride. The city, the New Jerusalem is the bride. Jesus Christ has redeemed a people to be His companion in the enjoyment of creation.

Mankind was created to look after and enjoy God's wonderful creation. We will be restored to that function. *"And they shall reign for ever and ever"*. We will reign over creation as those who care for it and ensure that it is beautiful for the King.

Revelation 22: 6 - 21

We have been permitted to glimpse into the glorious future. The prophecy now closes. We are reminded of the opening words of the prophecy. This is a message sent direct from the throne of God. It is absolutely reliable.

"Surely I am coming quickly!" As at the beginning we are reminded that the time is near (Revelation 1: 3). If the time is near then it may be in our lifetime. Therefore every generation should study and take seriously this prophecy. We are promised that whether or not the Lord returns we will be blessed by studying and keeping the words written here. The message contained in it is in fact for all time and every generation.

Watch

Jesus taught that the church should always be ready, alert, and watching (Matthew 24: 42, 25: 13, Luke 12: 35 – 40, 21: 34 – 36). By failing to watch the church has many times and in many places become conformed to this world. Nowhere else in scripture are the consequences of being conformed to this present evil age so clearly spelt out.

The blessing

The blessing which opened the prophecy is repeated here. *"Blessed is he who keeps the words of the prophecy of this book."* Revelation 1:3. Having got this far you will have read or heard these words. Now it is down to us to keep them.

Daniel was told to seal up the words of his prophecy until the end time (Daniel 12: 9). It is then that they would be understood. The message of Revelation is not sealed for it is not limited to the end of this age. It is a call to righteous living in every evil age.

The righteous are to persevere in their righteousness until He calls them home. They have heeded the words of this prophecy and are blessed by doing so.

In verse 19, there is another reminder that His coming is soon. We are to remain alert.

Jesus is coming both to reward the righteous, and as judge (Matthew 25: 21, 30). He initiates and concludes all that is in creation. Nothing exists independently of Him (John 1: 3).

Outside the city?

Outside the city is the lake of fire, where everyone whose name is not written in the Lamb's book of life, will be thrown. Jesus used the term 'Gehenna' often translated as '*Hell*' to describe this place (Matthew 10: 28). It was the name of the rubbish dump outside the city of Jerusalem, from which the smoke of bonfires was always rising. He also called Hell *"the outer darkness"* (Matthew 22: 13). Hell is so far from the presence of God that His light, which floods His creation, never reaches it.

This is the final warning of the Bible. God does not want anyone to go there. But if they continue in their rebellion they will be treated like rubbish consigned to a tiny, miserable, tormented, corner of His creation, destroyed and forgotten.

Jesus Himself bears witness to all that is written in this prophecy.

As *"the Root and Offspring of David"*, it is His right to claim the throne and reign as King. The *"Bright and Morning Star"*, heralds the dawn and the coming kingdom. Jesus, is like the Morning Star, an assurance to us that soon the day will dawn.

Finally the church unites with the Holy Spirit to say, *"Come"*. Revelation and the whole Bible close with an invitation. The gates are still open, now is the time to accept the invitation.

Such is the divine inspiration of this prophecy that it closes with a warning. Those who tamper with what it says will lose their place in the New Jerusalem. Both translators and interpreters beware; to alter the meaning and mislead the redeemed will be judged severely by God. The matters dealt with here lead either to eternal salvation or final punishment. Take care lest some are caused to stumble.

In conclusion Jesus Himself bears witness to all that is written in this prophecy.

"Surely I am coming quickly".

In reply the church affirms, *"Amen, even so, come Lord Jesus"*.

The eternal story now begins.
Will you be part of it?

Flee the Wrath to Come

To suffer the wrath of God and be thrown into the lake of fire is a horrific but preventable, tragedy. It is a tragedy which will affect not just a few but all who are living and have ever lived. Rarely is the alarm sounded. Frequently the wrong advice is being given.

The Bible assures us that God does not want anyone to suffer that fate. He has prepared a way of escape. But a way of escape is only effective if a person chooses to use it.

To be certain that you are going to be part of the main story and not face God's anger read the authors booklet 'Flee the Wrath to Come'. This booklet is available as a free download from:

https://www.trumpetsounds.net/wp-content/uploads/2018/01/Wrath-Booklet.pdf.

For a paper copy interested readers should contact the author via the Trumpet Sounds website: https://www.trumpetsounds.net/contact/

APPENDIX 1

WHAT DOES THE BIBLE MEAN BY ETERNAL LIFE?

"whoever believes in Him shall not perish but have eternal life."
John 3:16

One of the great travesties wrought on the Christian Church is the adoption of Greek thinking with regard to eternal life. The Greeks despised the body and elevated the spirit. From this thinking the world at large has the image of souls floating around on the clouds playing harps.

Many Christians think of heaven as divorced from this world. They believe that the future will be a spiritual existence alongside the angels surrounding the throne of God. Belief in a physical existence in a material world is looked on as cultic!

The Bible informs us that the present corrupted creation will be destroyed (2 Peter 3: 10). In its place there will be a new pure uncorrupted creation. It will be peopled by those who gladly obey their King. To live in the new earth we will be given new bodies. We will also be given access to the food that will enable us to live forever.

Adam and *Eve* were driven from the garden to prevent them eating of the tree of life (Genesis 3: 22, 23). Now everything has changed. The promise to those who overcome is, *"I will give to eat from the tree of life."* Revelation 2: 7

The tree of life is symbolic of Christ. We symbolically eat of that tree whenever we eat the bread and drink the wine to remember Christ's sacrifice. It reminds us that we will live because He sustains us. *"in Him all things consist."* Colossians 1:17 *"upholding all things by the word of His power."* Hebrews 1: 3. Everlasting life is life sustained by Christ. *Paul* said to the Athenians, *"for in Him we live and move and have our being."* Acts 17: 28.

The Westminster Shorter Catechism states *"Man's chief end is to glorify God and enjoy Him forever."* We will glorify Him through our obedience for that shows trust in His wisdom. We will enjoy Him as we are increasingly enthralled at the wonder of His creation. The vastness of those discoveries will never end.

Our present creation was once 'very good'. The new heavens and new earth will surpass the former glory. Even a fallen world is beautiful. How much more the new creation.

Here we will stop because we might get carried away and start to speculate what the new world will be like. I am sure that any speculation will fall far short of the reality of what is being prepared for us.

"No eye has seen, no ear has heard, nor has entered the heart of man, the things which God has prepared for those who love Him." 1 Corinthians 2: 9

The pardoned will enter through the gates into the paradise prepared for them.

APPENDIX 2

THE ANTICHRIST

At the end of this present age Satan will be permitted to perpetrate a great deception. He will be allowed to present to the world the man called, in 2 Thessalonians, *'the man of sin'*. God will not only permit this deception, He will use it so that all those who have already rejected the truth will be justly condemned by their own choice.

Old Testament references to this man are identified by taking three characteristics, *his blasphemy, the time of his appearing* and *his destruction by Jesus Christ*. In the Old Testament he is seen as a Middle Eastern tyrant who causes a time of great suffering for the Jews immediately prior to the return of Christ.

In Daniel 7 four beasts are seen rising from the great sea. From the fourth beast comes a little horn described as possessing eyes like a man and uttering great boasts. Verse 25 gives us more detail of this little horn's blasphemy. *"He will speak out against the Most High and wear down the saints of the Highest One, and he will intend to make alterations in times and in law; they will be given into his hand for time, times and half a time."* The little horn of this passage shares the three defining characteristic of the 'man of sin', his outspoken blasphemy, his existence at the end of time and his destruction by the personal intervention of God. The passage goes on to relate that the court will sit and this vile little horn will be annihilated and destroyed forever.

Daniel 8 provides more detail of this man. It points to the tyrant *Antiochus Epiphanes* as a forerunner of this person. Then towards the end of chapter 11 we come across another blasphemer. *"Then the king will do as he pleases, and will exalt himself above every god and will speak monstrous things against the God of gods;"* Daniel 11: 36. Up to this point chapter 11 has prophesied a conflict between *the King of the North* and the *King of the South* which lasted about 300 years. The conflict culminates with the rule of Antiochus Epiphanes.

At verse 36 there is a jump in time. The prophecy now closes with the time of trouble which precedes the resurrection. His blasphemy, the setting in time of the prophecy and his end all indicate that *the King of the North* is yet another name for the man of sin.

We turn to the book of Revelation for a much fuller description of this man.

Abaddon

Revelation 9 describes the release of a plague of demons from the pit. They are permitted to torment people for a period of time. *"And they had a king over them the angel of the bottomless pit, whose name in Hebrew is Abaddon, but in Greek he has the name Apollyon."* Revelation 9:11. Why is Abaddon mentioned by name?

His names mean *destruction* and *destroyer*. Both are terms used in connection with the end time oppressor of Israel (Isaiah 16: 4, *'shadad'* means destroyer or spoiler) and the *'man of sin'* (2 Thessalonians 2: 3 *'apoleia'* means *perdition* or *destruction*).

It is easy to overlook the significance of Abaddon. He is not released just to disappear from the scene but will become the principal character in much of what follows.

"The beast who you saw was, and is not and will ascend out of the bottomless pit and go to destruction." Revelation 17: 8. This verse confirms that Abaddon, released from the bottomless pit, will take on the identity of one who is called *'the beast'*. He has been imprisoned for centuries ready for this hour. As in 2 Thessalonians he is restrained until the time that God chooses to release him. He is described as *"was, is not, and yet is"*, which gives rise to the belief that we are reading about a man who once lived, is now dead, yet for a time will be resurrected.

In his book *'The Antichrist'* A. W. Pink, points to the Antichrist being *Judas Iscariot* resurrected. The only other person, besides the *'man of sin'*, to which scripture gives the title *'son of perdition'* (apoleia) is Judas Iscariot (John 17: 12). There are many who have become possessed by demons, but of Judas it is written that Satan entered into him (Luke 22: 3). When he died it was written *"that he might go to his own place."*

Acts 1: 25. Judas was not sent to the place of the dead but to a place reserved for him until the time that God will use him again. Although called to be among those privileged to be Jesus' close companions, he chose Satan instead of the Lamb of God. He has to bear the eternal consequence of his decision, as will all who follow him.

I believe that Abaddon will be resurrected to become the beast. *"And he was given a mouth speaking great blasphemies, and he was given authority to continue forty two months. Then he opened his mouth in blasphemy against God .... ."* Revelation 13: 5, 6. His blasphemy confirms that the beast is *'the man of sin'* who takes the name of God claiming to be God.

Many have difficulty with the idea of a man being kept imprisoned for centuries and then returned to life on earth. This however is the most straight forward interpretation of the Bible. In fact our faith is centred on the blessed hope that one day a man will return from heaven to gather us up to be with Him. Three times in Revelation similar words are used in reference to our Lord Jesus Christ, *"Who is and who was and who is to come"* Revelation 1: 8, *"Who was and is and is to come"* Revelation 4: 8, *"The One who is and who was and who is to come."* Revelation 11: 17. We believe that Jesus is. He is alive and will return.

Revelation specifically identifies the beast as the one *"that ascends out of the bottomless pit."* Revelation 11: 7. This is confirmed in Revelation 17:8 which is quoted above and adds *"that was and is not, and is about to come"*.

Living in a materialistic world, a concept such as this is difficult to comprehend. But then we must ask, do we really believe in the return of Christ and the rapture of the saints? It will happen because God has promised through Jesus to grant us eternal life, but it is still difficult to comprehend.

Only as God Permits

"The ten horns which you saw are ten kings who have received no

kingdom as yet, but they receive authority for one hour as kings with the beast." Revelation 17: 12. Both the beast of Revelation and the fourth beast of Daniel 7 have ten horns. In Daniel the ten horns are described but have no ascribed function. In Revelation we learn that they exist for a brief period of time. Their function is to give power and authority to the beast and to fulfil the purpose of God in destroying the harlot (Revelation 17: 15 – 17). All that happens is under the sovereign control of God. However much these monsters are inspired by Satan, their freedom to work their hateful destruction only exists to the extent God permits.

Will this man's reign be universal?

The answer from scripture is *possibly* but not *definitely.* Statements such as *"all the world marvelled and followed the beast."* Revelation 13: 3 and *"causes the earth and those who dwell in it to worship the first beast."* Revelation 13: 12 could be taken as meaning universal rule.

Elsewhere in scripture we find that similar phrases have a more limited scope. In the interpretation of **Nebuchadnezzar's** dream of the statue to be found in Daniel 2, both the first empire which was Babylon [Dan 2: 38] and the third empire, which was Greece [Dan 2: 39] are described in terms which we would interpret as reigning over the whole planet. We know from history that they only ruled what we today refer to as the Middle East. We find the same use of words in Ezra 1: 2 where Cyrus claims to rule over all the kingdoms of the earth. Luke 2: 1 records that *'all the world'* was to be registered. All the world here refers to the Roman Empire.

In the Sermon on the Mount of Olives, Jesus said that the gospel must be preached to all nations and also that His followers will be hated by all nations (Matthew 24: 9, 14). The word used is *'ethnos',* meaning *all ethnic groups.* The two statements go together. At the end of this age the gospel will be both preached and rejected, bringing down God's judgment on the world. There is no doubt that this applies to all peoples living on this planet.

In Revelation an angel announces that *"The kingdoms of this world have become our Lord's and even of His Christ, and He shall reign forever and ever"* (Revelation 11: 15). The word used for this world is *'kosmos'* which generally has a universal meaning covering the whole ordered world.

While of the beast it is written *"and all the earth marvelled after the beast"*. Here *'ge'* is used. Throughout Revelation the word 'ge' is usually translated *earth.* In many instances the context points to it being used to refer to the whole world. But the word can also mean a land, territory or region. We have to decide from the context and other scriptures what is intended in each instance.

"Then the fifth angel poured out his bowl on the throne of the beast and his kingdom became full of darkness; ..." Revelation 16: 10. *'Basileia'* translated *kingdom,* is usually used in the more limited context of a defined area. The Beast is described as having a specific realm.

"Now the beast which I saw was like a leopard, his feet were like a bear and his mouth like the mouth of a lion." Revelation 13: 2. This description of the beast takes us back to Daniel 7. In that chapter four beasts were described, one is like a lion, one like a bear, one like a leopard and a final dreadful beast. It connects the final empire of the beast to these former empires. The link could indicate that this final empire covers the same territory. That territory is the Middle East and depending on how Daniel 7 is interpreted, may also include Europe.

The Mark of Beast - *Revelation 13: 15 – 18*

The end of Revelation 13 introduces a topic which has been the cause of much speculation. Brands, tattoos, bar codes, micro chips and head bands have all been suggested as the mark. What it is will remain speculation until the time it comes into force. If the extent of the Beast's kingdom is limited it may be that only those within the kingdom will be caused to receive the mark.

A person who follows Christ is sealed with the Holy Spirit (2 Corinthians 1: 22, Ephesians 4: 30). The seal is a mark of ownership. The Christian no longer belongs to Satan and the kingdom of this world. He has been bought with the precious blood of Jesus and now belongs to the heavenly kingdom.

The mark of the beast is Satan's imitation of the seal of God. It identifies all who belong to him. Revelation 13 reveals a trinity of evil which mirrors the divine trinity of Father, Son and Holy Spirit. Satan models himself on the Father. The Beast is the incarnation of Satan imitating the Son. The false prophet imitates the ministry of the Holy Spirit. He deceives people into worshipping the Beast and seals those who have made that commitment.

Whatever the nature of the mark proves to be, accepting it will seal a person's destiny. Those who accept it will share the same fate as Satan. Revelation 14: 9 – 11 warns of the torment which will be suffered by all who receive the mark of the Beast.

Christians who refuse to worship the beast or receive his mark are in line to be beheaded. When Jesus returns they will be rewarded with the privilege of reigning with Him (Revelation 20: 4).

Thwarting Satan's rule

Satan intends to rule over the whole world. He will be permitted at the end of this age to use all his power to deceive mankind and bring that rule about. But we come against him in prayer backed by all the power of Jesus Christ. That sounds as if we are to pray against the will of God, which permits Satan to deceive the world. But God also has another purpose in mind. At the end of this age there will yet be a final harvest (Revelation 7: 14).

From scripture, we are assured that Jesus has the final victory. It is for the church to stand against the schemes of the devil and prevent them coming about. That is why he will hate us so much. The vigilant church, which has seen through the deception of Satan, will in suffering have the joy of seeing many saved. In the end they will witness Satan's defeat. We are confident because we follow the One who has already won the battle and is very soon going to reign victorious over all the earth. **Hallelujah.**

APPENDIX 3

THE NUMBER SEVEN IN REVELATION

Seven in scripture represents fullness or completion. The first example being found in Genesis when God rested from His work on the seventh day. The number seven is woven into scripture in such a way that it has been described as the DNA of the Bible.

Seven occurs in Revelation more times than in any other book of the Bible. Its occurrence so permeates this book that it is clearly intentional and therefore meaningful. In Revelation there are seven churches, seven Spirits of God, seven golden lampstands, seven stars, seven lamps of fire, seven seals on the scroll. The Lamb has seven horns and seven eyes. There are seven angels who stand before God with seven trumpets, seven thunders, seven thousand killed in the earthquake, seven heads with seven crowns on the dragon, seven angels with seven bowls of wrath and seven plagues, seven kings and seven mountains.

Besides the above there are seven mentions of each of the following; God's prophets, the earthquake, those who are blessed, Christ sword, Christ's blood, MY name, the Book of Life, prophecy, 'this book', judgment, right hand, the saints, God Almighty, the bottomless pit, 'come quickly' and Jesus lives. I leave readers to check out the above for themselves.

God has a plan for redeeming mankind which one day will come to completion. The great events which will close the present age are under His control. Once complete a new chapter for mankind will begin. Seven in Revelation assures us that God will bring His plans to completion.